Beyond Conflict

Transforming Relationships with Difficult Individuals

Brian Foster

Table of Contents

INTRODUCTION

Relationships are the threads that bind our lives' complicated tapestry together. They give us happiness, comfort, and a feeling of community. Yet, they can also be the source of frustration, pain, and conflict, especially when we encounter difficult individuals. These people challenge our patience, test our resilience, and push our emotional boundaries. We've all met people who seem to thrive on conflict, whether it be a controlling partner, toxic friend, demanding boss, or combative family member.

Discovering the core of interpersonal dynamics is what this book, "Beyond Conflict: Transforming Relationships with Difficult Individuals," is all about. More importantly, it guides how to turn these difficult relationships into opportunities for personal development, empathy, and even healing. It examines the profound effects that challenging people can have on our lives.

In the ensuing chapters, we will explore the psychology of challenging people, the causes of conflict, and the adverse effects of conflict on our well-being. We'll learn how to navigate these choppy waters with the help of self-reflection, effective communication, empathy, and healthy boundary-setting. You will learn how not just to survive but thrive in the company of challenging people through real-life experiences and helpful tactics.
"Beyond Conflict" extends an invitation to start on a life-changing path toward happier, more satisfying relationships. It serves as a manual for people looking for balance, kinship, and fortitude when dealing with the most challenging situations in life. Come with us as we explore the "Beyond Conflict" terrain and discover how

even the most challenging relationships can grow and heal.

CHAPTER I

Identifying Difficult Individuals

Understanding Difficult Individuals

We all encounter difficult people at some point in our lives. These people, who can range from the family member who never seems to be satisfied to the coworker who constantly challenges your ideas, can try our patience, stir up strong feelings, and throw off the balance in our relationships. Learning more about the psychology and behaviors of challenging people is essential to navigate these difficult interactions successfully. This comprehension serves as the cornerstone for constructing techniques for enhanced empathy, communication, and conflict resolution.

Above all, it's critical to understand that challenging people can take many different forms and aren't always "bad" people. Their distinct life experiences, beliefs, and coping mechanisms are the main causes of their frequently displayed behavioral patterns. Childhood traumas may have shaped some people's defensive or confrontational tendencies, while other people's difficult behavior may be a result of personality traits like narcissism or passive-aggressiveness. Recognizing that challenging people have multiple facets allows us to approach them with greater empathy and less criticism.

Understanding difficult individuals also requires an exploration of common traits and patterns that manifest across different personalities. Those who exhibit these characteristics may find it easy to point the finger at others, have a strong need for control, or be critical of others. Understanding these patterns can make it easier for us to anticipate challenging behavior and deal with it when it arises. For example, if you are aware of someone's tendency toward excessive criticism, you can emotionally and psychologically ready yourself to take constructive criticism without becoming defensive.

It's also critical to take triggers into account when analyzing the behavior of challenging people. Some may react strongly to certain situations or topics. By being aware of these triggers, we can facilitate more harmonious interactions and prevent unnecessary confrontations. To maintain a more tranquil atmosphere, you could decide to steer clear of a topic or approach it cautiously if you are aware that talking about it tends to upset a family member.

Difficult behavior frequently has deep psychological roots, so understanding these factors is essential. Unresolved emotional wounds in some difficult people can cause them to act defensively or aggressively. These actions could be a coping strategy they employ to shield themselves from more emotional pain. Recognizing this aspect can elicit compassion and encourage a more empathetic approach when dealing with such individuals.

Furthermore, social and cultural factors greatly impact how people behave. It's possible that difficult people grew up in settings where conflict was commonplace, which caused them to carry over these traits into adulthood. Difficult traits can arise due to family dynamics, cultural norms, and societal expectations. By being aware of these influences, we can approach difficult people with more cultural sensitivity and understand why they behave the way they do.

Conflict has a significant and pervasive effect on people, both the difficult people and those who interact with them. It's not only emotional and mental health that can suffer; physical health can also be compromised. Ongoing disputes can cause stress and tension, which can exacerbate several health problems, such as high blood pressure, compromised immune system, and a higher chance of developing chronic illnesses. Thus, realizing the negative effects of conflict on our well-being emphasizes how crucial it is to look for healthy strategies for resolving challenging interpersonal situations.

Conflict can harm our interpersonal relationships in addition to its physical effects. Repeated clashes with difficult individuals can lead to strained, damaged, or severed ties. These effects may affect not only the individuals directly involved but also families, groups, and communities. Comprehending the broader consequences of conflict emphasizes how important it is to devise efficient methods for handling and altering these difficult connections.

In conclusion, cultivating stronger, more harmonious relationships requires an intricate but crucial understanding of challenging people. We can approach difficult behavior with more empathy and less judgment when we acknowledge that difficult behavior can have different causes and that it frequently results from personality traits, past experiences, or coping mechanisms. We can more successfully anticipate and react to their behavior when recognizing common traits and triggers. Understanding the psychological, social, and cultural elements at work helps one understand why people act in certain ways. Furthermore, realizing the profound effects of conflict on our relationships and general well-being emphasizes how urgent it is to find healthy ways to handle these difficult situations. Enhancing our comprehension of challenging people helps us prepare for the life-changing process outlined in "Beyond Conflict: Transforming Relationships with Difficult Individuals."

Types of Difficult Individuals

The group of difficult people is diverse, with each member bringing with them a unique set of difficulties in their interpersonal interactions. It is essential to identify and comprehend the different kinds of challenging people to handle these difficult situations. We can create strategies for communication and conflict resolution by recognizing these unique personalities and behavior patterns, which will eventually help us turn these challenging relationships into more harmonious ones.

A common kind of challenging person is the "Critical Critic." These people frequently criticize others and don't hesitate to voice their unfavorable opinions. They often criticize ideas, actions, and even personal characteristics relentlessly. Working with a Critical Critic can be extremely difficult because they can be demoralizing and create a hostile environment. Empathizing with them can be facilitated by realizing that their criticism frequently results from control issues or personal insecurities. We can lessen conflict and promote more fruitful interactions by concentrating on constructive criticism and avoiding taking it personally.

An additional category of challenging individuals is the "Control Freak." These individuals have an intense desire for control in every aspect of their lives and may become controlling and domineering in relationships. They might micromanage tasks, dictate decisions, and resist compromise. They frequently act this way out of fear or insecurity, making them want to keep things in order and certain. We can handle these interactions more skillfully if we acknowledge their need for control. More balanced relationships can be facilitated by reducing conflicts with Control Freaks by establishing clear boundaries, being honest with one another, and looking for compromises.

Then there are those with a "victim mentality". These people frequently blame other people or outside factors for their problems and constantly view themselves as victims. They can be emotionally exhausting to be around and seldom accept responsibility for their choices or actions. Understanding that their victim mentality is often a defense mechanism can promote empathy. They can change their viewpoint and interact with others more healthily if personal accountability is encouraged and supportive assistance is provided without passing judgment.

"Passive-Aggressive" people are another difficult type. They indirectly express their hostility or resistance, often through sarcasm, backhanded compliments, or subtle sabotage. It can be challenging to deal with passive-aggressive people because their true motivations are never revealed. The first step in controlling passive-aggressive behavior is recognizing it. It is possible to lessen passive-aggressive tendencies and foster more sincere and positive interactions by addressing problems head-on, seeking clarification, and promoting direct communication.

People who are "narcissists" are a particularly tough type. They exhibit a grandiose sense of self-importance and an excessive need for admiration. Lacking empathy for others, narcissists frequently take advantage of or manipulate those around them to suit their own needs. Knowing that narcissism is a symptom of underlying insecurity can help explain their actions. During interactions with narcissists, maintaining your emotional wellbeing and minimizing conflicts can be achieved by setting boundaries, refraining from personal attacks, and concentrating on your needs.

"Manipulators" are people who manipulate others or themselves by lying, invoking guilt, or playing on emotions. They are skilled at exploiting vulnerabilities and often leave their targets feeling confused or emotionally drained. It is imperative to identify manipulative strategies to safeguard oneself from harm. By setting clear boundaries, looking for outside advice, and directly confronting manipulative behavior, one can lessen its influence and preserve better relationships.

"Aggressive Personalities" encompass individuals who display hostility, anger, or aggression as their default mode of interaction. To establish their dominance, they may be physically or verbally aggressive. Understanding that aggression often masks deep-seated insecurities or unresolved anger can provide insight into their behavior. Keeping oneself safe, reducing the intensity of conflicts, and promoting open communication when necessary are tactics for handling confrontations with aggressive people.

Lastly, "Drama Seekers" thrive on creating or amplifying conflicts and drama in their lives. They may exaggerate issues or cause unnecessary chaos because they enjoy being the center of attention. Handling these interactions can be made easier by acknowledging their need for excitement or approval. Refusing to participate in unnecessary drama, keeping a safe emotional distance, and focusing conversations on more positive topics are ways to lessen the adverse effects of drama seekers on relationships.

In conclusion, navigating difficult interpersonal relationships effectively requires understanding the different kinds of difficult people. Every kind has different difficulties, drives, and behavioral patterns. We can approach these unique personalities with more empathy and create plans to lessen conflict and promote peaceful relationships if we know the underlying causes of their challenging behavior. Ultimately, this knowledge allows us to change challenging relationships into ones marked by enhanced empathy, respect, and communication.

Recognizing Common Traits

In our journey to understand and navigate relationships with difficult individuals, one key aspect is the ability to recognize common traits that often manifest across various personalities. These common traits serve as valuable signposts, helping us identify and anticipate challenging behaviors and emotions. By becoming attuned to these recurring patterns, we can establish effective strategies for communication, conflict resolution, and personal growth in the face of difficult individuals.

One of the most prevalent common traits among difficult individuals is a tendency for criticism. They often have a critical eye for the actions, decisions, and characteristics of others. This criticism can be relentless and sometimes seem unwarranted or overly harsh. Recognizing this trait allows us to prepare ourselves emotionally and mentally for feedback that may be negative or challenging. It's essential not to take this criticism personally and to focus on the constructive aspects, if any, within their comments. By understanding that criticism often stems from their own insecurities or a need for control, we can approach such individuals with empathy and a willingness to engage in productive dialogue.

Another common trait is a need for control. Many difficult individuals intensely desire to control their environment, situations, or people. They may micromanage tasks, insist on their preferences, or resist compromise. This need for control often arises from fear or insecurity, and understanding this underlying motivation can help us navigate interactions with them. Setting clear boundaries and communicating openly is crucial to maintain a sense of agency and autonomy in such relationships. While meeting their demands may not always be possible, seeking compromises and common ground can alleviate conflicts and promote more balanced interactions.

A third common trait is a tendency to blame others for their problems. Difficult individuals often avoid taking responsibility for their actions or decisions, shifting the blame onto others or external circumstances. Recognizing this behavior pattern allows us to approach conversations with caution and empathy. Encouraging personal responsibility gently and supportively is important, rather than engaging in a blame game. We can promote personal growth and more accountable behavior by helping them acknowledge their role in conflicts or challenges.

Passive-aggressiveness is another trait frequently observed in difficult individuals. They indirectly express their hostility or resistance, often through sarcasm, backhanded compliments, or subtle sabotage. Dealing with passive-aggressive behavior can be perplexing because their true intentions remain concealed. Recognizing this trait is the first step in managing it effectively. When confronted with passive-aggressiveness, addressing issues openly, seeking clarity, and encouraging direct communication are essential. We can promote more honest and constructive interactions by fostering an environment where passive-aggressive tendencies are less likely to thrive.

A common trait that requires special attention is manipulation. Manipulative individuals use deceit, guilt-tripping, or emotional manipulation to achieve their goals or control others. They are skilled at exploiting vulnerabilities and often leave their targets feeling confused or emotionally drained. Recognizing manipulative tactics is essential to protect oneself from harm. Maintaining clear boundaries, seeking outside perspectives, and confronting manipulative behavior directly when it arises is crucial. By refusing to be manipulated and encouraging honest and transparent communication, we can reduce the influence of manipulative individuals in our lives.

Narcissism is another trait that stands out among difficult individuals. Narcissists exhibit a grandiose sense of self-importance and an excessive need for admiration. They often lack empathy for others and may exploit or manipulate those around them to meet their needs. Recognizing narcissism as a common trait allows us to approach interactions with caution. While it's challenging to change a narcissist's behavior, we can protect our own well-being by setting boundaries, avoiding personal attacks, and focusing on our needs during interactions with them.

Aggression, whether verbal or physical, is a common trait that poses significant challenges in relationships. Some difficult individuals have aggressive personalities and may use intimidation tactics to assert dominance. Recognizing this trait is crucial for personal safety. When dealing with aggressive individuals, it's important to de-escalate confrontations, seek support from authorities or professionals when necessary, and encourage open dialogue only in safe environments. By acknowledging the presence of aggression and taking appropriate measures, we can protect ourselves and promote a safer interaction.

"Drama Seeking" is another common trait that some difficult individuals exhibit. They thrive on creating or amplifying conflicts and drama in their lives, often enjoying being the center of attention. Recognizing their craving for excitement or validation can help us manage these interactions effectively. Maintaining emotional distance, refusing to engage in unnecessary drama, and redirecting conversations toward more constructive topics is important. We can maintain healthier and more peaceful relationships by minimizing their influence and not feeding into the drama.

In conclusion, recognizing common traits among difficult individuals is a valuable skill that enables us to navigate challenging interactions more effectively. These traits, such as criticism, control, blame-shifting, passive-aggressiveness, manipulation, narcissism, aggression, and drama-seeking behavior, serve as signposts to help us identify and anticipate difficult behavior patterns. Armed with this understanding, we can approach these relationships with greater empathy and awareness. Moreover, we can develop strategies to protect our well-being, set healthy boundaries, and promote more constructive and harmonious interactions. Ultimately, recognizing these common traits empowers us to navigate the complex terrain of difficult relationships with grace and resilience.

Case Studies

Case studies are powerful tools for understanding and navigating relationships with difficult individuals. These real-life scenarios provide insights into the complexities of human interactions, shedding light on the various personalities, behaviors, and dynamics at play. By examining these cases, we can glean valuable lessons, practical strategies, and a deeper understanding of transforming challenging relationships into more harmonious ones.

In the case of' The Critical Boss, ' Sarah, an employee, finds herself under a supervisor who constantly criticizes her work. This situation leaves Sarah demoralized and anxious, dreading each interaction with her boss. However, by employing strategies outlined in' Beyond Conflict, ' Sarah manages to turn the situation around. She practices self-reflection to understand her emotional triggers and sets boundaries by addressing her boss's criticism. Through effective communication, she expresses her concerns and requests constructive feedback. As a result, her boss becomes more aware of the impact of their behavior, leading to improved interactions and a healthier work environment. This case shows that even in difficult situations, positive change is possible.

Consider the case of' The Manipulative Friend.' Here, Alex finds himself in a friendship with Rachel, a master of manipulation who frequently twists situations to her advantage, often using guilt and emotional tactics. This leaves Alex feeling drained and conflicted after every interaction. But Alex doesn't let this situation continue unchecked. Armed with insights from' Beyond Conflict, ' he confronts Rachel with honesty and empathy, expressing his feelings and setting clear boundaries. He seeks support from other friends and remains firm in his resolve to maintain a balanced and respectful friendship. Over time, Rachel begins to understand the impact of her manipulative behavior and makes efforts to change, resulting in a more authentic and supportive friendship.

In a family setting, we encounter "The Blame-Shifting Sibling." In this case, Sarah's younger brother, Mark, consistently shifts blame onto others for his mistakes and mishaps, causing tension within the family. The case exemplifies the common trait of blame-shifting in difficult individuals. Mark's behavior creates frustration and conflict, as he avoids taking responsibility for his actions. Inspired by the insights from "Beyond Conflict," Sarah decides to address this issue proactively. She engages in open and empathetic communication with Mark, encouraging him to reflect on his behavior and its impact on the family. Sarah also involves their parents in the conversation, creating a supportive and collaborative environment for Mark to grow. Over time, Mark begins to acknowledge his role in family conflicts, leading to more harmonious relationships within the family.

In the workplace, "The Drama-Seeking Colleague" can be challenging. In this case, Tom works with a colleague, Lisa, who consistently stirs up drama and conflict within the team. Lisa enjoys being the center of attention and often exaggerates problems or creates unnecessary chaos. This case highlights the drama-seeking trait common among difficult individuals. Lisa's behavior disrupts team cohesion and productivity, creating a toxic work environment. Tom applies principles from "Beyond Conflict" to address this issue. He refuses to engage in unnecessary drama and encourages his team to focus on constructive solutions rather than getting caught up in Lisa's theatrics. Through Tom's leadership and the team's collective efforts, they manage to minimize Lisa's influence, leading to a more productive and drama-free work environment.

In conclusion, case studies offer insightful perspectives into the complexities of interacting with challenging people. These real-life scenarios illustrate the common traits and behavior patterns observed in such individuals, including criticism, control, blame-shifting, manipulation, narcissism, aggression, and drama-seeking tendencies. We gain practical knowledge and strategies for navigating these challenging interactions by examining these cases. Whether it's addressing a critical boss, dealing with a manipulative friend, managing a blame-shifting sibling, or handling a drama-seeking colleague, the principles outlined in "Beyond Conflict" provide a roadmap for transformation. These case studies remind us that we can turn difficult relationships into sources of growth, understanding, and connection with empathy, effective communication, boundaries, and support.

CHAPTER II

Understanding the Roots of Conflict

Exploring Personal Histories

The roots of conflict often run deep within the complexities of personal histories. To truly comprehend why individuals exhibit difficult behavior, one must embark on a journey into their past experiences, traumas, and the formative events that have shaped their worldviews. By delving into personal histories, we gain valuable insights into the origins of conflict, which, in turn, equip us with the empathy and understanding necessary for effectively navigating these challenging relationships.

Childhood experiences are pivotal in shaping an individual's behavior and attitude towards conflict. Many difficult individuals carry the scars of early life experiences that have left them emotionally wounded or insecure. These experiences may include childhood traumas, such as abuse, neglect, or the absence of positive role models. For instance, someone who grew up in an abusive household may develop aggressive tendencies or a fear of vulnerability, leading to defensive behavior in adulthood. Understanding the profound impact of childhood experiences allows us to approach difficult individuals with greater empathy. Recognizing that their behavior often stems from unresolved emotional wounds can help us de-escalate conflicts and foster a more compassionate atmosphere for communication and healing.

Furthermore, attachment styles formed in childhood significantly influence how individuals approach relationships and conflict in adulthood. According to attachment theory, our early interactions with caregivers influence our emotional reactions and coping mechanisms when faced with stress and conflict. Individuals with secure attachments tend to have more positive and resilient approaches to conflict, while those with insecure attachments may struggle with trust issues, abandonment fears, or emotional dependency. Recognizing an individual's attachment style provides critical insights into their behavior and reactions during conflicts. It allows us to tailor our communication and support strategies to meet their emotional needs effectively.

Cultural and familial influences are also instrumental in understanding the roots of conflict. Families and cultures often have specific norms, values, and expectations regarding behavior and communication. These norms can either exacerbate or mitigate conflict within relationships. For instance, a family that discourages open expression of emotions may produce individuals who struggle to communicate their feelings effectively, leading to passive-aggressive behavior or emotional suppression. Similarly, cultural norms surrounding assertiveness, hierarchy, and gender roles can significantly impact how conflict is perceived and managed. Recognizing these cultural and familial influences is vital in navigating relationships with difficult individuals. It enables us to appreciate the context in which their behavior developed and to approach conflicts with cultural sensitivity and awareness.

Personal histories also encompass individual traumas and adverse life events that can trigger or exacerbate conflict. Traumas, such as loss, betrayal, or personal crises, can leave emotional scars that influence an individual's behavior and reactions. For example, someone who experienced a painful breakup may become overly defensive or emotionally guarded in subsequent relationships, leading to conflicts with partners. Adverse life events, such as job loss or financial struggles, can also contribute to heightened stress levels and increased conflict within relationships. Understanding how past traumas and life events impact an individual's emotional state and behavior allows us to approach conflicts with greater compassion and patience. It encourages us to provide support and create an environment conducive to healing and resolution.

Psychological factors, including personality traits and coping mechanisms, further shape an individual's approach to conflict. Personality traits, such as narcissism, perfectionism, or neuroticism, can influence how individuals perceive and engage in conflicts. For instance, a person with narcissistic traits may struggle with empathy and prioritize their needs over others, leading to conflicts in interpersonal relationships. Coping mechanisms developed over time also play a significant role. Some individuals may have learned to cope with stress through avoidance or passive-aggressive behavior, which can exacerbate conflicts when triggered. Understanding these psychological factors helps us tailor our communication and conflict resolution strategies to address the specific challenges presented by difficult individuals.

In conclusion, exploring personal histories is fundamental in understanding the roots of conflict within interpersonal relationships. Childhood experiences, attachment styles, cultural and familial influences, traumas, adverse life events, personality traits, and coping mechanisms all contribute to an individual's behavior and reactions during conflicts. By delving into these personal histories, we gain valuable insights into the origins of difficult behavior, allowing us to approach these individuals with empathy and a deeper understanding of their motivations. Recognizing the profound impact of personal histories equips us with the tools necessary to navigate conflicts effectively, promote healing, and transform challenging relationships into ones characterized by improved communication, empathy, and mutual respect.

Psychological Factors at Play

Conflict is ubiquitous in human interaction, emerging from differences in beliefs, values, interests, and needs. Investigating the psychological causes and perpetuators of conflicts is crucial to properly addressing and resolving them. While the causes of conflicts are multifaceted, this section explores the critical psychological factors that contribute to the origins and persistence of conflicts, shedding light on the intricate web of human emotions, cognition, and behavior that shape our understanding of conflict dynamics.

One fundamental psychological factor underlying conflicts is perception. Individuals have different perspectives on the world, shaped by their experiences, biases, and beliefs. These differences in perception can cause people to misunderstand and misinterpret the intentions and actions of others, which can inevitably spark conflicts. For instance, in a workplace setting, a manager may perceive an employee's criticism as insubordination, while the employee views it as constructive feedback. Such perceptual discrepancies can escalate conflicts if not addressed with sensitivity and open communication. To mitigate conflicts rooted in perception, individuals must acknowledge the subjectivity of their perspectives and strive to consider alternative viewpoints empathetically.

Emotions play a significant role in conflict dynamics. Emotions like anger, fear, and frustration can intensify conflicts, leading to impulsive reactions and a communication breakdown. For example, a heated argument between spouses may escalate due to both parties' overwhelming anger. Furthermore, unresolved emotional wounds from past experiences can resurface in current conflicts, amplifying negative emotions and perpetuating cycles of discord. To manage the impact of emotions in conflicts, individuals must develop emotional intelligence, which involves recognizing, understanding, and regulating their own emotions, and also empathizing with the emotions of others. By doing so, individuals can defuse emotionally charged conflicts and create space for constructive dialogue.

Cognitive biases also contribute significantly to the roots of conflict. Confirmation bias, for instance, leads individuals to seek information confirming their preexisting beliefs and dismissing contradictory evidence. In a political debate, for example, two individuals may hold opposing views and selectively interpret facts to reinforce their own perspectives, leading to an impasse. Another cognitive bias, the fundamental attribution error, causes people to attribute others' negative actions to inherent character flaws while attributing their own negative actions to situational factors. This bias can fuel conflicts by reinforcing negative stereotypes and attributions. To counter cognitive biases, individuals must engage in critical thinking and self-reflection, actively questioning their assumptions and considering alternative explanations.

Self-interest and competition are often psychological factors at the heart of conflicts, particularly in resource disputes, economic competitions, and interpersonal rivalries. People naturally seek to fulfill their own needs and goals, sometimes at the expense of others, leading to conflicts of interest. For instance, in a corporate environment, two employees vying for a promotion may engage in subtle sabotage or rivalry. Recognizing and addressing conflicts stemming from self-interest require promoting collaboration, negotiation, and compromise. By finding common ground and mutually beneficial solutions, conflicts rooted in self-interest can be transformed into opportunities for cooperation.

Communication breakdowns are another psychological factor that contributes to conflicts. Ineffective communication can lead to misunderstandings, misinterpretations, and escalated tensions. Poor communication skills, such as active listening and empathetic expression, can hinder the resolution of conflicts. In a family setting, for instance, a parent and a teenager may have difficulty communicating about curfew rules, resulting in frustration and arguments. To address conflicts rooted in communication breakdowns, individuals must invest in improving their communication skills, fostering an environment of openness, and ensuring that both parties feel heard and understood.

Identity and group dynamics can also play a substantial role in conflicts. People often derive a sense of identity and belonging from their affiliations with various groups, such as cultural, religious, or political communities. Conflicts can arise when these identities are threatened or when individuals perceive their group as superior to others. For example, ethnic or religious tensions can escalate when individuals view their group's interests as more important than those of others. To mitigate conflicts arising from identity and group dynamics, promoting intergroup empathy and cooperation is essential. Recognizing the shared humanity and common goals that transcend group boundaries can help break down barriers and foster understanding.

Psychological defenses, such as denial, projection, and rationalization, can obstruct conflict resolution by inhibiting individuals from taking responsibility for their actions or acknowledging their contributions to a conflict. In a workplace dispute, for instance, a colleague may deny any wrongdoing and blame the other party, hindering the resolution process. To address conflicts rooted in psychological defenses, individuals must engage in self-reflection and self-awareness, acknowledging their own roles in conflicts and taking responsibility for their actions. By doing so, they can pave the way for honest dialogue and resolution.

The psychological phenomenon of escalation can exacerbate conflicts over time. Escalation occurs when each party responds to the other's actions with increasingly hostile or aggressive behaviors, resulting in a destructive cycle. For example, in a neighborly dispute over a property boundary, one party may retaliate by building a fence that encroaches further onto the other's land, prompting a tit-for-tat escalation. To prevent escalation, individuals must recognize the danger of retaliatory actions and seek to de-escalate conflicts through communication, compromise, and seeking common ground.

Moreover, power imbalances can significantly affect the dynamics of conflicts. When one party possesses more power or resources than the other, conflicts can become inherently unequal, making resolution challenging. For instance, employees may face a powerful employer in labor disputes, limiting their bargaining power. Addressing conflicts rooted in power imbalances requires efforts to level the playing field, promote fairness, and ensure all parties have an equal voice and opportunities for redress.

In conclusion, conflicts are complex and multifaceted phenomena influenced by many psychological factors. These factors, including perception, emotions, cognitive biases, self-interest, communication breakdowns, identity and group dynamics, psychological defenses, escalation, and power imbalances, contribute to the origins and persistence of conflicts. Understanding and addressing these psychological factors are essential steps in effectively resolving conflicts and fostering empathy, cooperation, and peace. By recognizing the intricate interplay of human emotions, cognition, and behavior, individuals and societies can work towards transforming conflicts into opportunities for understanding, growth, and positive change.

Social and Cultural Influences

In our quest to comprehend the roots of conflict within interpersonal relationships, we must recognize the significant role played by social and cultural influences. The attitudes, beliefs, and behaviors that people exhibit regarding conflict are greatly influenced by the social and cultural environments in which they are raised, as well as the prevailing norms and values. To understand why people exhibit difficult behavior during conflicts, it is crucial to delve into these social and cultural factors, as they provide invaluable insights into the origins of conflict and guide us in navigating these challenging relationships effectively.

Society often imparts specific expectations and norms regarding appropriate behavior and communication, particularly within the context of conflict. These societal influences can either exacerbate or mitigate conflicts, depending on the values and practices upheld. For instance, cultures or societies prioritizing individualism may encourage direct and assertive communication during conflicts, whereas those emphasizing collectivism may value harmony and indirect communication to preserve relationships. These cultural differences in conflict resolution styles can lead to misunderstandings and frustrations when individuals from diverse backgrounds interact. Recognizing and respecting these societal norms is crucial for effective conflict management. It allows us to appreciate the context in which difficult behavior arises and adapt our communication strategies to bridge cultural gaps and promote understanding.

The way that conflicts are handled and resolved is also greatly influenced by the social construct of gender roles and expectations. Gender norms often prescribe specific roles and behaviors for men and women, both in private and public spheres. Men may be encouraged to adopt assertive and dominant communication styles, while women may be socialized to prioritize harmony and compromise. These gendered expectations can manifest in conflicts, with men being more prone to confrontational behavior, and women more inclined towards passive-aggressiveness or emotional expression. These gender dynamics can create challenges in communication and conflict resolution, especially in mixed-gender relationships. Recognizing and challenging these gender stereotypes is essential for promoting equality and facilitating healthier conflict interactions.

Cultural diversity within a society further compounds the complexity of interpersonal conflicts. In multicultural societies, individuals often navigate relationships with people from diverse cultural backgrounds, each bringing their unique perspectives and communication styles to the table. Misunderstandings and conflicts may arise when individuals from different cultures interpret behaviors or expressions differently. For instance, a direct communication style may be seen as assertive in one culture and rude in another. In such cases, cultural sensitivity becomes paramount. Understanding the cultural context in which an individual operates and appreciating their communication style can foster cross-cultural understanding and mitigate conflicts. It enables individuals to navigate diverse relationships with empathy and respect.

Social hierarchies and power dynamics also shape conflict behavior. In societies with rigid hierarchies or power imbalances, individuals in positions of authority may exhibit dominance and control, leading to conflicts with those in subordinate positions. Recognizing these power dynamics is essential for understanding the roots of conflict. It allows individuals to challenge unfair power structures and advocate for equality in their relationships. Conversely, in more egalitarian societies, conflicts may arise from a perceived lack of hierarchy or decision- making authority. Understanding these nuances of power dynamics enables individuals to navigate conflicts with a more balanced approach and promote healthier relationships.

Cultural collectivism and individualism significantly influence how individuals perceive conflicts within their families. In collectivist cultures, the family unit often takes precedence over individual desires, leading to conflicts that revolve around issues of duty, honor, and tradition. In contrast, individualistic cultures may prioritize personal autonomy and independence, resulting in conflicts related to personal choices and boundaries. Recognizing these cultural orientations helps individuals appreciate the motivations and perspectives of family members. It enables them to navigate familial conflicts with empathy and respect for cultural values.

Moreover, societal and cultural attitudes towards emotions also play a pivotal role in conflict dynamics. Some cultures may encourage emotional expression and vulnerability to resolve conflicts, while others may promote emotional restraint and stoicism. These cultural attitudes can significantly impact how individuals react and respond during conflicts. Recognizing these variations in emotional expression allows for more effective conflict resolution. It enables individuals to adapt their communication styles to align with cultural expectations while still fostering open and honest dialogue.

In conclusion, social and cultural influences are integral to understanding the roots of conflict within interpersonal relationships. Society imparts specific expectations and norms regarding conflict resolution, often shaped by cultural, gender, and power dynamics. These influences can lead to misunderstandings, frustrations, and challenges in communication. To navigate these conflicts effectively, individuals must recognize and respect these societal and cultural norms, challenge gender stereotypes, appreciate cultural diversity, understand power dynamics, and adapt their communication styles accordingly. By doing so, they can foster cross-cultural understanding, promote equality, and navigate conflicts with empathy, ultimately transforming challenging relationships into ones characterized by improved communication, empathy, and mutual respect.

CHAPTER III

The Impact of Conflict on Individuals

Emotional and Mental Health

Conflict, whether in the workplace, within families, or in personal relationships, profoundly impacts the emotional and mental health of individuals involved. The emotional toll of ongoing conflicts can be debilitating, often leading to increased stress, anxiety, depression, and an array of different mental health issues. Understanding the intricate relationship between conflict and emotional/mental health is essential in recognizing the true cost of unresolved disputes and provides the groundwork for implementing strategies to mitigate these negative effects.

One of the most immediate and palpable impacts of conflict on emotional health is heightened stress. The body's stress response, often called the "fight or flight" reaction, is triggered during conflicts, resulting in a rise in the level of stress hormones such as cortisol. Prolonged exposure to such stress can harm one's emotional well-being, leading to heightened irritability, difficulty concentrating, and sleep disturbances. Moreover, the chronic stress resulting from unresolved conflicts can contribute to long-term health issues, including hypertension, heart disease, and a weakened immune system. Recognizing the connection between conflict and stress is essential in addressing its emotional toll. It underscores conflict resolution's importance in reducing chronic stress and protecting emotional health.

Anxiety is another common emotional response to conflict. Uncertainty, fear of negative outcomes, and the anticipation of further conflicts can all contribute to heightened anxiety levels. This anxiety can manifest as generalized anxiety disorder, panic attacks, or specific phobias related to the conflict. Individuals may constantly worry about the next conflict or experience physical symptoms such as rapid heart rate, shortness of breath, or sweating. Understanding the connection between unresolved conflicts and anxiety emphasizes the need for timely conflict resolution. It encourages individuals to seek strategies for managing anxiety, such as mindfulness techniques or therapy, to mitigate the emotional impact of conflict.

Conflict can also be a trigger for depression or exacerbate preexisting depressive symptoms. The constant stress, negative emotions, and feelings of helplessness that often accompany conflicts can lead to a downward spiral of low mood and hopelessness. Extended periods of experiencing such emotional distress may lead to the development of clinical depression, which is marked by persistent sadness, disinterest in activities, alterations in eating or sleeping habits, and even suicidal or self-harming thoughts. Recognizing the potential link between conflict and depression is critical for individuals seeking to protect their emotional well-being. It underscores the significance of seeking professional help when needed and implementing strategies for coping with depression, such as therapy or medication.

Furthermore, unresolved conflicts can strain relationships and create feelings of isolation and loneliness. People who are experiencing emotional distress as a result of ongoing conflicts may isolate themselves from others out of fear of criticism or confrontation. Isolation and loneliness can exacerbate existing emotional and mental health issues, as social connections are essential for emotional well-being. Recognizing the impact of conflict on relationships and the resulting isolation is vital. It highlights the need for open and honest communication to repair damaged relationships and rebuild social support networks.

One less visible but equally impactful consequence of conflict on emotional health is the erosion of self-esteem and self-worth. Repeated negative interactions, criticism, and blame from conflicts can lead individuals to internalize these messages, damaging their self-image. Feelings of inadequacy and worthlessness can be exacerbated by this negative self-perception, which can result in emotional and mental health problems including depression as well as anxiety. It is critical to understand how subtle the deterioration of one's self-worth is when there are unresolved conflicts involved. It emphasizes how crucial it is to cultivate and preserve a positive self-image via counseling, self-compassion, and relationships that are affirming.

Unresolved disputes can also prolong an endless cycle of psychological and emotional suffering. The emotional toll that conflict takes on people can make it harder for them to control their stress, anxiety, and depression. This, in turn, can lead to further conflicts, creating a self-perpetuating cycle of emotional distress. Recognizing this cycle is vital for breaking the pattern and seeking strategies for both conflict resolution and emotional self-care. It highlights the importance of proactive conflict management to prevent the compounding of emotional and mental health issues.

The impact of conflict on emotional and mental health is not limited to individuals directly involved; it can also affect bystanders and witnesses. In families, for instance, children who witness ongoing conflicts between their parents may experience emotional trauma and develop behavioral or emotional problems. In workplaces, conflicts among colleagues can create a hostile and stressful environment for all employees, leading to decreased job satisfaction and increased turnover. Recognizing the ripple effect of unresolved conflicts underscores the importance of addressing conflicts quickly and effectively. It emphasizes the need for organizations and communities to provide support as well as resources for individuals affected by conflicts, including access to counseling or mental health services.

In conclusion, conflict's emotional and mental health impact is substantial and far-reaching. Conflict contributes to heightened stress, anxiety, depression, and a range of emotional as well as mental health issues. It can strain relationships, erode self-esteem, perpetuate cycles of distress, and affect not only those directly involved but also bystanders and witnesses. Recognizing the profound toll of unresolved conflicts on emotional and mental health underscores the urgency of prioritizing conflict resolution as a means to protect emotional well-being. It encourages individuals to seek support and resources for managing the emotional effects of conflict, from therapy and mindfulness techniques to building positive self-esteem and fostering healthy relationships. Ultimately, understanding the complex relationship between conflict and emotional/mental health is the first step towards mitigating these negative effects and creating a path towards emotional resilience and well-being.

Physical Health

While the consequences of conflict are often discussed in emotional and psychological terms, it is equally important to recognize the significant impact that conflicts can have on an individual's physical health. The stress, tension, and negative emotions that accompany unresolved conflicts can take a toll on the body, leading to an array of physical health issues. Understanding the connection between conflict and physical health is essential, as it highlights the importance of effective conflict resolution in maintaining overall well-being and quality of life.

One of the most immediate physical effects of unresolved conflicts is increased stress. When individuals experience conflict, their bodies respond by releasing stress hormones, like cortisol and adrenaline. Long-term exposure to these hormones may trigger a variety of physical symptoms, such as tense muscles, shallow breathing, elevated blood pressure, and an accelerated heart rate. These physiological responses can be harmful if they persist over time. High blood pressure, in particular, is a risk factor for heart disease and stroke, emphasizing the need to address conflict-related stress for the sake of physical health.

In addition, chronic stress brought on by ongoing disputes can impair immunity, leaving people more vulnerable to disease. Stress hormones suppress the immune response, making it harder for the body to fight off infections. Consequently, individuals who experience frequent conflicts may find themselves falling ill more often or taking longer to recover from illnesses. This weakened immune system can lead to a cascade of health problems, including frequent colds, infections, and prolonged recovery from injuries or surgeries. Recognizing the connection between unresolved conflicts and compromised immunity highlights the importance of stress management and conflict resolution as essential components of maintaining physical health.

Unresolved conflicts can also disrupt sleep patterns, leading to sleep disturbances and insomnia. The heightened stress and emotional turmoil associated with conflicts can make it difficult for individuals to relax and fall asleep. Sleep is essential for maintaining physical health because it helps the body's systems heal and regenerate. Ongoing disputes can cause chronic sleep deprivation, which can result in a variety of health problems, such as exhaustion, deteriorated cognitive function, and a higher chance of developing long-term illnesses like diabetes and obesity. Understanding the impact of conflicts on sleep underscores the importance of addressing conflict-related stress to protect one's physical well-being.

Chronic pain is another physical health issue that can result from unresolved conflicts. The stress and tension experienced during conflicts can exacerbate physical pain conditions, such as headaches, muscle tension, and gastrointestinal discomfort. Individuals may find that their pain symptoms worsen or become more frequent when conflicts remain unresolved. Recognizing the connection between unresolved conflicts and physical pain emphasizes the need for comprehensive pain management strategies that address both the emotional and physical aspects of pain.

Furthermore, conflicts can lead to harmful coping behaviors that have detrimental effects on physical health. Some individuals may turn to substances like alcohol, tobacco, or unhealthy eating habits as a means of coping with stress and emotional distress resulting from conflicts. These behaviors can lead to addiction, weight gain, and other physical health problems. Understanding the link between conflicts and harmful coping mechanisms highlights the importance of seeking healthier ways to regulate stress and emotions, such as exercise, or therapy.

The impact of unresolved conflicts on physical health extends beyond the individual directly involved. For example, in a family, conflicts between parents may be detrimental to their children's physical health. Parental conflicts can cause stress and tension in children, which can cause sleep disturbances, emotional distress, as well as developmental problems. In workplaces, conflicts among colleagues can create a hostile and stressful environment, leading to physical health problems for all employees. Recognizing the broader impact of conflicts on physical health underscores the importance of addressing conflicts promptly and effectively. It emphasizes the need for organizations and communities to give support and resources for individuals affected by conflicts, including access to stress management programs and conflict resolution strategies.

In conclusion, the impact of conflict on physical health is significant and multifaceted. Conflict-related stress can lead to a range of physical health issues, including elevated blood pressure, weakened immunity, sleep disturbances, chronic pain, and harmful coping behaviors. Furthermore, conflicts can have a detrimental impact on the physical health of bystanders, such as family members and colleagues. Recognizing the connection between unresolved conflicts and physical health emphasizes the urgency of prioritizing conflict resolution as a means to protect physical well-being. It encourages individuals to seek support and resources for managing the physical effects of conflict, from stress management techniques to pain management strategies. Ultimately, understanding the complex relationship between conflict and physical health underscores the need for a holistic approach to well-being that addresses both the emotional and physical aspects of conflicts in order to maintain overall health and quality of life.

Interpersonal Relationships

Interpersonal relationships are at the core of human existence, shaping our emotional well-being, personal growth, and overall quality of life. However, conflicts within these relationships can have a profound impact on individuals, often leading to strained bonds, emotional distress, and lasting consequences. To understand the full extent of the impact of conflict on individuals, it is crucial to explore how these disputes affect their interpersonal relationships and the complex dynamics that arise as a result.

Conflicts within interpersonal relationships can strain bonds and erode trust. Trust is a basic component of any healthy relationship, whether it's between partners, friends, family members, or colleagues. When conflicts arise, trust can be compromised as individuals may feel betrayed, hurt, or let down by those they care about. This erosion of trust can create a lasting emotional scar, making it difficult for individuals to fully open up and trust others in the future. Recognizing the role of conflict in undermining trust highlights the importance of addressing disputes with care and empathy, aiming for resolutions that rebuild trust rather than further damaging it.

Moreover, conflicts within relationships often lead to heightened emotional distress. When disagreements escalate into hurtful or emotionally charged exchanges, individuals can experience intense emotions such as anger, sadness, frustration, and anxiety. These emotional responses can take a toll on one's overall well-being and mental health, contributing to stress-related illnesses and long-term emotional distress. Understanding the emotional impact of conflicts within relationships underscores the need for effective conflict resolution techniques that prioritize emotional well-being and consider the emotional toll on individuals involved.

Conflict can also disrupt communication patterns within relationships, making it difficult for individuals to express themselves effectively. In the heat of a disagreement, communication often breaks down as individuals may become defensive, accusatory, or avoidant. Misunderstandings can arise, and important issues may go unresolved. This breakdown in communication can perpetuate conflicts and create a cycle of misunderstanding and frustration. Recognizing the role of conflict in communication breakdowns highlights the need for improved communication skills and strategies that promote constructive dialogue and understanding.

Furthermore, conflicts within relationships can lead to feelings of isolation and loneliness. When disagreements persist and lead to emotional distance, individuals may feel isolated from their loved ones. The fear of judgment, further conflicts, or rejection can discourage individuals from seeking emotional support or sharing their feelings. This isolation can exacerbate emotional distress and create a sense of loneliness even within the context of a relationship. Recognizing the potential for isolation resulting from conflicts emphasizes the significance of creating a secure and supportive spaces within relationships where individuals can express themselves without fear of judgment or reprisal.

Conflicts can also alter power dynamics within relationships, leading to imbalances that affect the well-being of those involved. For instance, in abusive relationships, conflicts can result in power and control tactics, further perpetuating cycles of abuse and manipulation. Recognizing the potential for conflicts to exacerbate power imbalances is crucial for promoting healthy relationships and safeguarding the well-being of individuals in vulnerable situations. It underscores the importance of seeking support and resources to address power imbalances and protect one's safety and autonomy.

Family relationships, in particular, can bear a heavy burden when conflicts arise. Conflicts within families can disrupt the sense of unity and support that family members rely on. Sibling rivalries, parental conflicts, or disputes over family matters can create divisions that impact family dynamics for years to come. Recognizing the potential for long-lasting rifts within families resulting from conflicts highlights the importance of addressing family disputes with care and empathy, prioritizing the preservation of familial bonds and support networks.

In the workplace, conflicts among colleagues can lead to a hostile and stressful environment that affects productivity, job satisfaction, and overall well-being. When conflicts persist, employees may feel overwhelmed, anxious, or demotivated, leading to decreased job performance and job-related stress. Recognizing the impact of workplace conflicts on individuals underscores the need for conflict resolution strategies and workplace policies that prioritize a healthy and respectful work environment.

In conclusion, the impact of conflict on individuals goes beyond the immediate emotional distress, extending to the core of their interpersonal relationships. Conflicts can strain bonds, erode trust, disrupt communication, foster isolation, and alter power dynamics within relationships. These consequences have far-reaching implications for individuals' personal growth, emotional well-being, and the overall quality of life. Recognizing the complex dynamics at play in the wake of conflicts within relationships highlights the importance of effective conflict resolution techniques that prioritize empathy, understanding, and the preservation of healthy interpersonal bonds. Ultimately, understanding the multifaceted impact of conflict on interpersonal relationships underscores the need for proactive efforts to foster constructive dialogue, maintain trust, and prioritize emotional well-being within the context of relationships, both personal and professional.

CHAPTER IV

Strategies for Self-Reflection

Assessing Your Own Behavior

Self-reflection is a potent tool for personal growth and development. It involves taking a step back and critically examining one's thoughts, actions, and behaviors. In assessing your behavior, self-reflection becomes a key process for gaining insights into your actions, motivations, and their impact on yourself and others. By engaging in self-reflection, you can identify areas for improvement, enhance self-awareness, and make positive changes in your behavior. In this section, we will explore strategies for self-reflection and the benefits they offer in assessing your own behavior.

One fundamental aspect of self-reflection is the ability to cultivate self-awareness. Self-awareness is the capacity to observe and understand your thoughts, emotions, and actions as they occur. It is a critical first step in assessing your own behavior because it allows you to recognize patterns and triggers that influence how you react in various situations. Self-awareness helps you understand why you behave the way you do, enabling you to take more conscious and intentional actions.

To enhance self-awareness, you can regularly set aside time for introspection. This could involve journaling your thoughts and emotions, meditating, or simply taking moments of quiet reflection. During these periods, ask yourself questions like "Why did I react that way?" or "What were my underlying feelings in that situation?" These inquiries encourage self-awareness by prompting you to delve into the motivations and emotions that drive your behavior.

Another valuable strategy for assessing your own behavior through self-reflection is seeking external feedback. Others' perspectives can provide insights into your actions and behaviors that you might not be aware of. Asking for constructive feedback from friends, family members, or colleagues can help you better understand how your behavior impacts those around you. When seeking feedback, be open to receiving both positive and negative comments, as they can all contribute to your growth and self-improvement.

Moreover, engaging in self-reflection requires a willingness to confront your own biases and assumptions. We all have ingrained beliefs and prejudices that influence our behavior. These biases can be unconscious, making examining them essential to avoid actively perpetuating harmful actions or behaviors. Assessing your own behavior means questioning your assumptions and considering how they might be affecting your interactions with others. It entails stepping outside your comfort zone to challenge preconceived notions and embrace a more open-minded and empathetic perspective.

A powerful aspect of self-reflection is its role in identifying areas for improvement and personal growth. By critically examining your behavior, you can pinpoint areas where you may be falling short or where you can make positive changes. Self-reflection encourages self-accountability, empowering you to take ownership of your actions and work towards personal development. For instance, if you find that you tend to react impulsively in stressful situations, self-reflection can lead you to explore relaxation techniques or stress management strategies to improve your responses.

Moreover, self-reflection can be a valuable tool in developing emotional intelligence. Emotional intelligence entails recognizing and managing your emotions effectively, as well as understanding and empathizing with the emotions of others. Assessing your own behavior allows you to gain insights into how emotions influence your actions and interactions. It enables you to identify emotional triggers and develop strategies for responding more thoughtfully and empathetically in challenging situations.

In addition to personal growth, self-reflection is vital in enhancing your relationships with others. When you assess your own behavior, you become more attuned to how your actions affect those around you. This heightened awareness lets you to make conscious choices contributing to healthier and more positive relationships. For example, suppose you recognize that you tend to interrupt others during conversations. In that case, self-reflection can lead you to practice active listening and cultivate better communication skills, ultimately improving your relationships.

Furthermore, self-reflection can be a source of empowerment. It empowers you to take control of your behavior and make intentional choices aligned with your values and goals. Instead of reacting impulsively or falling into negative patterns, self-reflection allows you to pause and consider your actions consciously. This empowerment can result in increased self-esteem and also confidence as you gain greater control over your behavior and its impact on your life and relationships.

However, it is essential to acknowledge that self-reflection can be challenging and may bring uncomfortable truths to the surface. Confronting your own shortcomings or recognizing harmful behaviors can be difficult. It requires a degree of vulnerability and self-compassion. It's crucial to approach self-reflection with an attitude of self-acceptance, understanding that growth and change are ongoing processes. Be kind to yourself, recognizing that everyone makes mistakes and has areas for improvement.

In conclusion, assessing your own behavior through self-reflection is a valuable and transformative practice. It cultivates self-awareness, encourages personal growth, and empowers you to make intentional choices in your actions and interactions. By seeking external feedback, challenging your biases and assumptions, and embracing self-accountability, you can better understand your behavior and its impact on yourself and others. Through self-reflection, you enhance your self-awareness and emotional intelligence and contribute to more positive and fulfilling relationships, both personally and professionally. Self-reflection is a powerful tool for personal development and self-improvement, enabling you to lead a more intentional and purposeful life.

Identifying Triggers

Self-reflection is a journey of self-discovery and personal growth that involves examining one's thoughts, emotions, and behaviors. A crucial aspect of effective self-reflection is identifying triggers – the events, situations, or stimuli that prompt certain emotional or behavioral reactions. Understanding your triggers is fundamental because it allows you to gain insights into your responses, manage emotions, and make informed decisions about your behavior. In this section, we will explore strategies for identifying triggers and the benefits they offer in the context of self-reflection.

It is essential to start by paying close attention to your emotional responses in various situations to identify triggers. Emotions serve as powerful indicators of what triggers you. When you experience intense emotions like anger, sadness, frustration, or anxiety, take a moment to reflect on the circumstances leading up to those feelings. Ask yourself questions like "What happened just before I felt this way?" or "What thoughts were going through my mind?" These inquiries help you pinpoint the triggers that elicit strong emotional reactions.

Self-awareness is a foundational skill in identifying triggers. By cultivating self-awareness, you become more attuned to your internal emotional landscape. You can recognize the subtle shifts in your mood and emotional state, allowing you to catch triggers as they occur. Self-awareness can be developed through practices including mindfulness meditation, journaling, or simply taking moments of quiet reflection. The more you practice self-awareness, the better equipped you become at identifying triggers and understanding your emotional responses.

It is also valuable to explore your past experiences and patterns of behavior when identifying triggers. Sometimes, triggers are deeply rooted in past traumas, insecurities, or unresolved issues. Examining your personal history and the recurring themes in your life can provide clues about what triggers you. For instance, if you notice a pattern of feeling anxious in situations where you perceive a lack of control, this may be linked to past experiences that have left you feeling powerless. Recognizing these patterns allows you to address underlying issues and develop strategies to manage your triggers more effectively.

Additionally, seeking external feedback can be instrumental in identifying triggers. Others may observe patterns in your behavior or emotional responses that you are unaware of. Trusted family members, friends, or colleagues can offer valuable insights by pointing out situations where you seem particularly reactive or emotional. When receiving feedback, be open to different perspectives and be willing to explore whether certain events or circumstances consistently trigger specific reactions.

It is important to note that triggers can be both external and internal. External triggers are events or situations in your environment that prompt emotional or behavioral responses. Examples of external triggers might include criticism from a coworker, traffic congestion during your commute, or news headlines that evoke strong emotions. Internal triggers, on the other hand, are thoughts, memories, or beliefs that generate emotional reactions. These internal triggers may be rooted in past experiences, self-doubt, or negative self-talk. Identifying both external and internal triggers is essential for a comprehensive understanding of your emotional responses.

Another effective strategy for identifying triggers is keeping a trigger journal. This involves documenting your emotional reactions and the events or circumstances leading up to them. In your journal, record the triggering incident's date, time, location, and details. Describe your emotional response, thoughts, and any physical sensations you experienced. Over time, reviewing your trigger journal can reveal recurring patterns and common triggers. It allows you to identify trends and better understand what provokes your emotional responses. Furthermore, recognizing the physiological signs of being triggered is essential. Triggers often manifest in physical sensations such as increased heart rate, muscle tension, or shallow breathing. By paying attention to these bodily signals, you can become more aware of when you are being triggered, even before the emotional response fully unfolds. These physical cues serve as early warning signs, prompting you to pause and engage in self-reflection before reacting impulsively.

Once you have identified triggers, the next step is to assess their impact on your behavior and well-being. Not all triggers are harmful or negative; some may be linked to positive emotions or motivations. It is essential to differentiate between triggers that enhance your life and those that contribute to distress or unproductive behaviors. Understanding the consequences of triggers helps you prioritize which ones to address and manage.

Managing triggers effectively involves a combination of strategies. For instance, you can develop coping mechanisms to deal with triggers that elicit negative emotions. These may include mindfulness practices, deep breathing exercises, or seeking social support when needed. You can also work on reframing your thoughts and beliefs related to certain triggers and challenging unhelpful or irrational thinking patterns.

Moreover, creating a trigger plan can be beneficial. A trigger plan involves premeditated strategies for managing specific triggers when they arise. For example, if you know that criticism triggers feelings of insecurity and defensiveness, your trigger plan might involve reminding yourself of your strengths and seeking clarification when receiving feedback. Having a plan in place allows you to respond more consciously and constructively to triggers, reducing their negative impact on your behavior and emotional well-being.

In conclusion, identifying triggers is crucial to self-reflection and personal growth. It empowers you to understand the events, situations, or stimuli that prompt emotional or behavioral reactions. By cultivating self-awareness, exploring your past experiences, seeking external feedback, and keeping a trigger journal, you can gain valuable insights into your triggers. Recognizing both external and internal triggers, along with their physiological signs, allows you to take control of your emotional responses and behavior. Effective trigger management strategies, such as coping mechanisms and trigger plans, enable you to respond to triggers more intentionally and constructively. Identifying and managing triggers is a potent tool for enhancing emotional intelligence, self-awareness, and overall well-being, contributing to personal growth and healthier relationships with others.

Building Emotional Intelligence

Emotional intelligence, often called EQ, is crucial to personal growth and social success. It encompasses the capacity to recognize, understand, manage, and influence one's own emotions and those of others. In the context of self-reflection, building emotional intelligence is a valuable endeavor that enhances self-awareness, interpersonal relationships, and overall well-being. This section will explore strategies for building emotional intelligence through self-reflection and its benefits in navigating the complexities of human emotions.

Self-reflection serves as the foundation for building emotional intelligence. It involves taking a step back to examine your thoughts, emotions, and behaviors without judgment. By engaging in self-reflection, you can gain a deeper understanding of your emotional responses and the patterns that govern them. For example, when you experience a strong emotional reaction, self-reflection prompts you to explore that emotion's underlying causes and triggers. This practice allows you to recognize recurring emotional patterns and the events or situations that provoke them.

One essential aspect of building emotional intelligence is cultivating self-awareness. Self-awareness entails recognizing and understanding your own emotions as they occur. Through self-reflection, you can become more attuned to your emotional state, pinpointing the specific emotions you are experiencing and their intensity. This heightened self-awareness enables you to take a step back from your emotions, providing you with the space to evaluate and manage them effectively. Self-awareness is a cornerstone of emotional intelligence because it is the basis for all other EQ competencies.

Regular self-reflection practices are key to enhancing self-awareness. These practices can include journaling your thoughts and emotions, practicing mindfulness meditation, or simply setting aside moments of quiet reflection. During these periods, focus on exploring your emotional experiences. Ask yourself questions like "What am I feeling right now?" or "Why am I feeling this way?" These inquiries encourage self-awareness by prompting you to delve into your emotional landscape and gain a more comprehensive understanding of your inner world.

Another fundamental aspect of building emotional intelligence is empathy for yourself and others. Self-reflection can deepen your sense of empathy by helping you connect with your own emotional experiences and, in turn, relate better to the emotions of others. When you take the time to understand and empathize with your own emotions, you develop the capacity to do the same for those around you. Empathy allows you to recognize the emotions of others, even when they are not explicitly expressed, and respond with compassion and understanding.

Moreover, self-reflection encourages self-regulation, which is another crucial component of emotional intelligence. Self-regulation involves managing your emotional responses effectively and making intentional choices about how to express your feelings. When you engage in self-reflection, you become more adept at identifying your emotional triggers and recognizing when your emotions may be leading you to react impulsively or negatively. This awareness empowers you to pause and consider your response consciously. For example, if you identify a tendency to become defensive when receiving criticism, self-regulation enables you to choose a more constructive response, such as seeking clarification or feedback.

Furthermore, self-reflection is a powerful tool for improving your social skills, another dimension of emotional intelligence. Social skills encompass the ability to navigate social situations, communicate effectively, as well as build positive relationships with others. When you engage in self-reflection, you gain insights into your communication style, interpersonal patterns, and the impact of your behavior on others. This awareness permits you to adapt your communication to better connect with those around you. For instance, if you recognize that you tend to interrupt others during conversations, self-reflection can lead you to practice active listening and foster better communication skills.

Building emotional intelligence through self-reflection also involves recognizing and challenging your own biases and assumptions. We all carry ingrained beliefs and prejudices that can influence our emotions and behavior. These biases may be unconscious, making it essential to actively examine them to avoid perpetuating harmful actions or behaviors. Self-reflection prompts you to question your assumptions and consider how they might be affecting your interactions with others. It encourages you to challenge preconceived notions and embrace a more open-minded and empathetic perspective.

In addition to self-awareness and empathy, another critical component of emotional intelligence is motivation. Motivation involves being driven by intrinsic goals and values rather than external rewards. Self-reflection can assist you in connecting with your inner motivations and align your actions with your values. By examining your emotional responses and behavior in various situations, you can identify what truly matters to you and what drives your actions. This self-awareness empowers you to make decisions and pursue goals that are in alignment with your values, leading to greater fulfillment and motivation in life.

Furthermore, building emotional intelligence through self-reflection contributes to better conflict resolution skills. Conflict is an inherent part of human relationships, and emotional intelligence plays a pivotal role in effectively navigating and resolving conflicts. When you are emotionally intelligent, you can recognize your own emotions and those of others during conflicts, enabling you to address the underlying issues rather than getting caught up in emotional reactions. Self-reflection helps you identify your triggers and patterns of behavior during conflicts, allowing you to respond more thoughtfully and empathetically. It enables you to engage in productive communication and seek mutually beneficial solutions.

In conclusion, building emotional intelligence through self-reflection is a valuable and transformative practice. It enhances self-awareness, empathy, self-regulation, social skills, and motivation. By engaging in regular self-reflection practices, you become more adept at recognizing your emotional patterns, understanding your triggers, and managing your emotional responses effectively. This heightened emotional intelligence enables you to relate better to others, navigate social situations with ease, and build healthier relationships. It empowers you to make choices aligned with your values, fostering greater fulfillment and motivation in life. Ultimately, building emotional intelligence through self-reflection is a journey of personal growth and self-improvement that leads to enhanced well-being and more harmonious interactions with others.

CHAPTER V

Effective Communication

Active Listening

Effective communication is essential for strong bonds in both personal and professional contexts. Active listening is a vital element of effective communication. Being able to actively listen entails more than just hearing what is being said; it also entails giving the speaker your whole attention, comprehending their viewpoint, and answering thoughtfully. In this section, we will explore the concept of active listening, its importance in effective communication, and strategies for developing this vital skill.

Active listening is an intentional and focused form of listening that requires your full attention and presence. When you engage in active listening, you are not merely waiting for your turn to speak or thinking about your response; you are genuinely absorbing and processing what the speaker is saying. This process involves hearing the words and recognizing the speaker's emotions, intentions, and underlying messages.

One fundamental element of active listening is giving your undivided attention to the speaker. This means putting aside distractions and respecting the speaker's thoughts and feelings. In today's fast-paced world, with constant technological interruptions, active listening can be challenging but is all the more crucial. To practice this skill, make a conscious effort to eliminate distractions when engaging in a conversation. Put away your phone, close your laptop, and focus on the person speaking.

Furthermore, active listening involves nonverbal cues that convey your attentiveness. Maintaining eye contact with the speaker signals your interest and engagement. Your body language, such as nodding or leaning in slightly, demonstrates your openness and receptivity. These nonverbal cues reinforce your commitment to understanding the speaker's perspective and contribute to building trust and rapport in the conversation.

Another critical aspect of active listening is using verbal cues to demonstrate your engagement and understanding. These cues include paraphrasing, reflecting, and clarifying. Paraphrasing involves summarizing the speaker's words in your own words, demonstrating that you are processing the information and seeking clarification. For example, you might say, "So, if I understand correctly, you're saying that..." Reflecting involves mirroring the speaker's emotions, allowing them to feel heard and validated. For instance, you might respond with, "It sounds like you're feeling frustrated about..." Clarifying involves seeking additional information or elaboration when something is unclear. You can say, "Could you please explain that further?"

Active listening also entails asking open-ended questions to encourage the speaker to share more deeply. Open-ended questions prompt thoughtful responses and invite the speaker to express their thoughts and feelings. These questions typically begin with words like "how," "what," "why," or "tell me about." For instance, you might ask, "Can you tell me more about your experience?" or "How do you feel about this situation?"

Empathy is a cornerstone of active listening. Empathetic listening involves understanding the speaker's perspective and genuinely feeling and connecting with their emotions. When you practice empathy, you convey compassion and support, making the speaker feel heard and valued. To develop empathy, try to put yourself in the speaker's shoes, imagining how they might feel and their experience. Acknowledge and validate their emotions, even if you don't necessarily agree with their perspective.

Another important aspect of active listening is suspending judgment. Often, individuals are quick to form opinions or make assumptions during a conversation, which can hinder effective communication. Active listening requires setting aside your judgments and biases, allowing the speaker to express themselves freely. Remember that your goal is to understand their perspective, not necessarily to agree with it. By suspending judgment, you create a safe and open space for dialogue.

Active listening is not only limited to verbal communication; it also entails paying attention to nonverbal cues. Nonverbal communication includes facial expressions, gestures, tone of voice, and body language. These cues provide valuable insights into the speaker's emotions and intentions. For example, a person's body language may indicate discomfort or defensiveness, even if their words suggest otherwise. Paying attention to nonverbal cues gives you a more comprehensive understanding of the speaker's message.

Additionally, patience and self-control are needed for active listening. While it may be easy to jump in and start giving answers or interrupting during a conversation, doing so can make it more difficult for the other person to fully express themselves. Rather, engage in active listening by waiting for the other person to complete their sentence and express their emotions before answering. This patience shows that you appreciate their viewpoint and facilitates better communication.

Apart from its function in establishing rapport and trust, active listening plays a crucial role in resolving conflicts. When conflicts arise, individuals often have strong emotions and differing viewpoints. Active listening allows both parties to express themselves fully and feel heard, which is crucial in finding common ground and working toward a resolution. By practicing active listening during conflicts, you can create a more constructive and empathetic dialogue, increasing the possibility of reaching a mutually satisfactory outcome.

Moreover, active listening is an essential skill in leadership and teamwork. A culture of open communication is fostered and team members' opinions are valued by effective leaders who actively listen to their team members. Team members who feel heard and understood are more likely to be engaged and motivated. Active listening also promotes collaboration, as it encourages the sharing of diverse perspectives and ideas. In team settings, practicing active listening contributes to better decision-making and problem-solving.

Active listening is not limited to professional contexts; it is equally valuable in personal relationships. When you listen to your loved ones actively, you strengthen your connections and deepen your understanding of one another. It allows you to offer support, empathy, and validation, which are crucial components of healthy relationships. In personal relationships, active listening promotes intimacy and helps navigate challenging conversations with care and respect.

In conclusion, active listening is a critical ability in successful communication. It means focusing entirely on the speaker, demonstrating your interest with both verbal and nonverbal clues, and exercising patience and empathy. In personal and professional settings, active listening helps to establish positive relationships, resolve conflicts, and develop trust. By honing your active listening skills, you can become a more effective communicator, a supportive friend or partner, a skilled leader, and a valuable team member. Ultimately, active listening is a powerful tool for enhancing understanding, empathy, and connection in all aspects of life.

Nonviolent Communication

Healthy relationships, fruitful collaborations, and the resolution of conflicts all depend on effective communication. In our increasingly interconnected world, the capacity to communicate effectively with empathy and understanding is more crucial than ever. Nonviolent Communication (or NVC), also known as compassionate communication, is a communication model and skill set that aims to foster connection, resolve conflicts, and promote understanding without resorting to aggression or hostility. This section will explore the concept of Nonviolent Communication, its key principles, and its importance in effective communication.

Developed by Marshall B. Rosenberg, Nonviolent Communication is a model that centers around the idea that all human beings have the capacity for compassion and empathy. NVC seeks to facilitate communication that connects individuals on a deeper level, transcending judgments and blame. At its core, NVC is grounded in the belief that universal human needs drive all human actions and speech and that conflicts arise from unmet needs rather than from inherent malice or ill intent.

One of the fundamental principles of Nonviolent Communication is the concept of observation without evaluation. In NVC, observations are concrete and specific descriptions of observable behavior, rather than judgments or interpretations. By focusing on observations, communicators can avoid making assumptions about others' intentions or character, which often leads to defensiveness and resistance. Instead of saying, "You're always late; you're so inconsiderate," an NVC practitioner might say, "I noticed that you arrived 15 minutes after our agreed-upon time for our meeting."

In addition to observations, NVC emphasizes the importance of expressing feelings rather than thoughts disguised as feelings. Many people tend to mix thoughts, evaluations, and interpretations with their feelings, which can lead to confusion and miscommunication. NVC encourages individuals to identify and express their genuine emotions. For example, instead of saying, "I feel like you don't care about my opinions," an NVC practitioner might say, "I feel hurt and frustrated when I perceive that my opinions aren't valued."

Another key element of Nonviolent Communication is the articulation of needs. Needs are universal human requirements that drive our behavior. Identifying and expressing our needs allows us to connect with others on a fundamental level because needs are something we all share. NVC encourages individuals to be aware of their own needs and to express them clearly and directly. For example, instead of saying, "I need you to stop interrupting me," an NVC practitioner might say, "I have a need for uninterrupted time to express my thoughts."

Nonviolent Communication also emphasizes the use of requests instead of demands. Demands can feel coercive and can trigger resistance in others, whereas requests invite collaboration and understanding. NVC encourages individuals to make requests that are specific, actionable, and respectful of others' autonomy. For example, instead of saying, "You must complete this task by tomorrow," an NVC practitioner might say, "Could you please complete this task by tomorrow if it's possible for you?"

Empathy is a central component of Nonviolent Communication. Empathy involves actively listening to others and striving to understand their feelings and needs. NVC practitioners are encouraged to offer empathetic responses that acknowledge the emotions and needs expressed by others. By demonstrating empathy, communicators can create an environment of trust and openness. For example, in response to someone expressing frustration, an NVC practitioner might say, "It sounds like you're feeling really frustrated because your need for clarity isn't being met."

Furthermore, Nonviolent Communication recognizes that conflicts often arise from unmet needs. Instead of engaging in blame or accusation, NVC encourages individuals to view conflicts as opportunities for understanding and connection. When conflicts occur, NVC practitioners are advised to engage in open and empathetic dialogue to uncover the unmet needs on both sides and seek mutually satisfactory solutions.

The effectiveness of Nonviolent Communication lies in its ability to foster connection and understanding even in the midst of conflict or disagreement. By adhering to the principles of NVC, individuals can communicate more authentically and empathetically, creating a space where needs and emotions can be expressed without judgment or criticism. This approach enhances personal relationships and proves valuable in professional settings and conflict resolution scenarios.

Nonviolent Communication can lead to more profound connections and improved intimacy in personal relationships. When individuals communicate their feelings and needs with honesty and vulnerability, it fosters a sense of trust and emotional closeness. NVC enables partners to understand each other on a deeper level and work together to meet each other's needs. Instead of escalating conflicts or resorting to blame, couples can engage in compassionate communication that seeks to resolve issues collaboratively.

In the workplace, Nonviolent Communication can transform the dynamics of teams and organizations. Effective communication is essential for successful collaboration, problem-solving, and productivity. When individuals practice NVC in the workplace, it promotes a culture of respect and empathy. Employees feel heard and valued, which can boost morale and job satisfaction.

Furthermore, conflicts are more likely to be resolved constructively, leading to improved working relationships and more effective teamwork.

Nonviolent Communication also plays a significant role in conflict resolution and peacemaking efforts. In situations of conflict, whether on a personal, community, or international scale, NVC can be a powerful tool for de-escalation and finding common ground. By focusing on shared human needs rather than opposing positions, NVC enables parties in conflict to explore mutually beneficial solutions and build bridges of understanding. It has been used successfully in mediation and peacebuilding initiatives worldwide.

Additionally, nonviolent communication adheres to restorative justice tenets. The goal of restorative justice is to make amends for wrongdoing by emphasizing the needs of both offenders and victims, as opposed to concentrating only on punitive measures. NVC can facilitate restorative justice processes by enabling both victims and offenders to express their feelings and needs in a safe and empathetic environment. This approach promotes accountability, healing, and reconciliation.

While Nonviolent Communication offers numerous benefits in enhancing understanding and resolving conflicts, it is not without its challenges. Practicing NVC requires high self-awareness, emotional intelligence, and empathy. Setting aside judgments and engaging in empathetic listening can be difficult, especially in emotionally charged situations. Moreover, some individuals may resist or misinterpret NVC, viewing it as overly passive or permissive.

In conclusion, Nonviolent Communication is a powerful and transformative approach to effective communication. Grounded in principles of empathy, authenticity, and respect for universal human needs, NVC fosters connection, resolves conflicts, and promotes understanding without resorting to aggression or hostility. By adhering to the principles of observation without evaluation, expressing feelings rather than thoughts disguised as feelings, articulating needs, making requests instead of demands, and demonstrating empathy, individuals can enhance their personal relationships, excel in the workplace, and contribute to conflict resolution and peacemaking efforts. While NVC may present challenges in its practice, its potential for transforming communication and promoting a more compassionate and empathetic world makes it a valuable skill worth cultivating.

Conflict Resolution Techniques

Human interaction will inevitably lead to conflict because of divergent viewpoints, needs, and interests. The way disagreements are resolved can have a big influence on cooperation, relationships, and general wellbeing. Constructive conflict resolution is heavily dependent on effective communication. In this section, we will explore various conflict resolution techniques that promote understanding, collaboration, and peaceful resolution of conflicts.

One widely recognized conflict resolution technique is active listening. Active listening involves fully engaging with the speaker, understanding their perspective, and providing meaningful responses. When individuals engage in active listening during a conflict, it demonstrates a genuine willingness to understand the other person's point of view. This technique includes giving your full attention, maintaining eye contact, and using verbal cues like paraphrasing, reflecting, and clarifying. By actively listening, individuals can uncover both parties' underlying concerns and emotions, facilitating a deeper understanding of the conflict.

Empathy is another critical component of effective conflict resolution. To be empathetic, one must try to put themselves in the other person's position and comprehend their needs and feelings. It is a powerful tool for fostering connection and compassion during a conflict. By empathizing with the emotions and needs of the other party, individuals can create an atmosphere of understanding and mutual respect. This technique involves acknowledging the other person's feelings and needs, even if one does not agree with their perspective. It can lead to a sense of validation and reduce defensiveness, opening the door to more constructive dialogue.

Communication skills such as assertiveness and clarity are also essential in conflict resolution. Assertiveness involves expressing one's needs, feelings, and perspectives honestly and respectfully. It is about finding a balance between being passive and aggressive, asserting oneself without infringing on others' rights. Assertive communication allows individuals to articulate their concerns and boundaries clearly, preventing misunderstandings and diffusing tensions. Clarity in communication ensures that messages are conveyed accurately, minimizing the potential for misinterpretation or confusion. It involves using straightforward language and avoiding vague or ambiguous statements.

Collaboration is a conflict resolution technique that emphasizes working together to find mutually beneficial solutions. Collaborative conflict resolution recognizes that conflicts often arise from differing interests or needs. Instead of viewing the conflict as a win-lose situation, collaboration seeks win-win outcomes. This technique involves brainstorming creative solutions, considering the perspectives and needs of both parties, and finding compromises that address the underlying issues. Collaboration promotes cooperation and strengthens relationships, as it demonstrates a commitment to finding solutions that benefit everyone involved.

In some cases, reframing the conflict can be a valuable technique in conflict resolution. Reframing involves shifting the perspective on the conflict to view it in a more positive or constructive light. It does not deny the conflict's existence but seeks to reframe it as an opportunity for growth or understanding. For example, reframing a disagreement between coworkers as a chance to improve communication and teamwork can change how the conflict is perceived. Reframing can assist people in shifting their attention from dwelling on the negative aspects of the conflict to finding solutions.

A neutral third party is involved in mediation, a formal conflict resolution process, to help parties communicate and come to a resolution. Due to their training in conflict resolution, mediators are qualified to effectively lead the process. They guarantee that both sides can voice their opinions, establish a controlled and safe space for open conversation, and help to identify points of agreement.

Mediation is particularly useful in situations where direct communication between the conflicting parties has broken down or become hostile. It offers an impartial and objective perspective to help resolve disputes.
Negotiation is a technique commonly used in conflict resolution, especially in professional and legal contexts. Negotiation involves a give-and-take process where parties work together to find mutually acceptable solutions. It may involve compromise, trade-offs, and concessions, aiming to reach an agreement that addresses the conflict's core issues. Effective negotiation requires effective communication skills, including active listening, assertiveness, and empathy. It is necessary to approach negotiations with a collaborative mindset and with a willingness to find common ground.

In some cases, the use of third-party experts or specialists can be a valuable conflict resolution technique. These experts may provide technical knowledge, expertise, or insights that help resolve the conflict. For example, bringing in a subject matter expert can provide clarity and guidance in a dispute over a technical project. The involvement of experts can facilitate informed decision-making and contribute to finding solutions that are based on facts and expertise.

Time can also be a crucial conflict resolution technique. Sometimes, conflicts can be resolved or diffused simply by allowing time for emotions to settle and perspectives to evolve. Taking a break from a heated discussion or postponing a decision can allow individuals to reflect and reconsider their positions. Time can be especially valuable when emotions are running high, and impulsive reactions may worsen the conflict. During this cooling-off period, individuals can engage in self-reflection and perspective-taking.

Furthermore, compromise is a well-known conflict resolution technique that involves finding middle ground between opposing positions. Compromise acknowledges that both parties may need to make concessions to reach a mutually agreeable solution. While compromise may not result in getting everything one wants, it often leads to an acceptable resolution to both parties. Compromising requires open communication and a willingness to find common ground. It can be particularly effective when multiple issues exist in the conflict, and each party is willing to make trade-offs.

Finally, the utilization of alternative dispute resolution methods, such as arbitration or collaborative law, can be effective conflict resolution techniques in specific situations. These methods offer structured processes for resolving conflicts outside of the traditional court system. Arbitration involves a neutral arbitrator who hears both parties' arguments and makes a binding decision. Collaborative law involves a cooperative approach, where an attorney represents each party, and all parties work together to find a resolution without litigation. These alternative methods can be faster and less adversarial than traditional litigation.

In conclusion, effective communication is pivotal in resolving conflicts constructively. Various conflict resolution techniques, including active listening, empathy, assertiveness, clarity, collaboration, reframing, mediation, negotiation, third-party experts, time, compromise, and alternative dispute resolution methods, can help individuals address conflicts to promote understanding, cooperation, and peaceful resolution. By applying these techniques, individuals can navigate conflicts with greater skill and effectiveness, improving relationships, teamwork, and overall well-being.

CHAPTER VI

Building Empathy

Empathy Exercises

Empathy is a fundamental human ability that enables us to understand and share the emotions as well as perspectives of others. It forms the basis of meaningful connections, effective communication, and compassionate relationships. Empathy benefits individuals in their personal lives and is crucial in fostering understanding and cooperation in society at large. Building and enhancing empathy can be a valuable endeavor, and there are various empathy exercises that individuals can practice to develop and strengthen this essential skill.

One effective empathy exercise is active listening. Active listening involves offering your full attention to the speaker, without interruptions or judgment, and genuinely understanding their perspective and feelings. To practice active listening, individuals should focus on the speaker's words, maintain eye contact, and provide verbal cues such as nodding or paraphrasing to show they are engaged and attentive. Active listening requires suspending one's own thoughts and reactions and fully immersing oneself in the speaker's world. This exercise enhances empathy by fostering understanding and creates a secure and supportive space for individuals to express themselves.

Another empathy exercise involves perspective-taking. Perspective-taking encourages individuals to put themselves in another person's shoes and consider the world from their point of view. This exercise can be practiced by reflecting on a situation or experience from someone else's perspective, imagining their emotions, thoughts, and motivations. By engaging in perspective-taking, individuals can gain insights into the feelings and needs of others, which can lead to greater empathy and a more profound understanding of different viewpoints.

Empathy journaling is a valuable exercise that encourages individuals to record their empathetic experiences and reflections. To practice empathy journaling, individuals can write about situations where they felt a strong connection with someone else's emotions or where they successfully understood and supported another person. Journaling allows individuals to revisit their empathetic experiences, reflect on what contributed to their empathetic responses, and identify areas for improvement. It also provides a record of growth in empathy over time.

Another empathy exercise that can be particularly powerful is volunteering or engaging in acts of kindness. Volunteering is taking an active part in endeavors that benefit or support others. Examples of such endeavors include helping a friend in need or volunteering at a nearby charity. A helpful hand, a kind word, or a supportive gesture can all be considered acts of kindness. Engaging in these activities benefits others and cultivates empathy by allowing individuals to connect with the experiences and needs of those they are helping. It reinforces the idea that empathy is not just a passive feeling but an active force for positive change.

Additionally, storytelling is a compelling empathy exercise. Sharing personal stories and experiences can bridge the gap between individuals and create a deeper understanding of each other's lives. Storytelling allows people to connect on a human level by highlighting common emotions, challenges, and aspirations. By listening to and sharing stories, individuals can relate to the joys and struggles of others, fostering empathy and building connections.

Art and creative expression can also be powerful tools for building empathy. Participating in creative activities like writing, painting, or acting allows individuals to explore emotions and perspectives beyond their own. Creating art can be a therapeutic and reflective process that encourages individuals to step into different emotional states and understand the depth of human experiences. Art can serve as a medium for empathy, both in the creation and appreciation of artistic works.

Furthermore, mindfulness meditation is an effective exercise for enhancing empathy. Being totally present in the moment, without distraction or judgment, is a requirement of mindfulness meditation. It inspires people to develop compassion for both themselves and other people as well as to objectively observe their thoughts and feelings. People can increase their awareness of their own emotions and their sensitivity to the emotions of those around them by practicing mindfulness meditation. This practice fosters empathy by encouraging individuals to approach themselves and others with compassion and understanding.

Engaging in structured empathy-building activities, such as empathy workshops or role-playing exercises, can be beneficial. These activities provide a structured framework for individuals to practice empathetic responses and communication skills. Role-playing exercises, for instance, allow individuals to step into different roles and perspectives, simulating real-life scenarios that require empathy and active listening. Workshops provide guidance and opportunities for participants to learn and practice empathy in a supportive environment.

Additionally, reading literature and novels can be a rich source of empathy-building experiences. Literature exposes readers to diverse characters, cultures, and experiences, permitting them to immerse themselves in different worlds and viewpoints. By empathizing with the fictional characters in a story, readers can develop empathy for the experiences and challenges they encounter. Reading broadens one's understanding of human complexity and fosters empathy by exploring a range of emotions and perspectives.

Educational programs that focus on empathy development can be particularly effective in building this skill. Schools and organizations can implement curricula that teach empathy as a core competency. These programs often include activities, discussions, and exercises that help individuals understand the importance of empathy, practice it in various contexts, and apply it in their daily lives. By embedding empathy education into formal settings, individuals can develop empathy as an integral part of their personal and social growth.

Finally, self-reflection is a foundational empathy exercise. Individuals can set aside time for self-reflection to explore their own emotions, beliefs, and biases. By understanding their own inner world, individuals can become more aware of their own emotions and responses, which can in turn enhance their ability to empathize with others. Self-reflection encourages individuals to confront their own prejudices and assumptions and consider how these factors may influence their interactions with others.

In conclusion, empathy is a critical skill that fosters understanding, compassion, and connection with others. Various empathy exercises, including active listening, perspective-taking, empathy journaling, volunteering, storytelling, art and creative expression, mindfulness meditation, structured activities, literature, educational programs, and self-reflection, can help individuals develop and strengthen their empathy. By practicing these exercises, individuals can cultivate empathy as a powerful force for promoting harmonious relationships, effective communication, and a more compassionate and understanding society. Building empathy is an ongoing journey of personal growth and self-improvement that contributes to greater empathy in the world.

Developing a Compassionate Mindset

Empathy is a basic human quality that promotes compassion, connection, and healthy interpersonal interactions. It is having the capacity to understand and share the feelings and viewpoints of others. Building and enhancing empathy is a worthwhile endeavor that can lead to more meaningful interactions, improved communication, and a deeper understanding of diverse experiences. One powerful approach to developing empathy is by cultivating a compassionate mindset. Compassion is the willingness to recognize suffering in others and take action to alleviate it. By nurturing a compassionate mindset, individuals can enhance their empathetic responses and contribute to a more empathetic and caring world.

A compassionate mindset begins with self-compassion. Self-compassion involves treating oneself with the same kindness and understanding that one would offer to a friend in times of difficulty or suffering. Developing self-compassion is a critical step in building empathy because it allows individuals to recognize their own humanity and vulnerabilities. When individuals are compassionate toward themselves, they are less likely to judge and criticize themselves harshly, which can interfere with their ability to empathize with others. Instead, self-compassion creates a foundation of self-acceptance and emotional resilience that enables individuals to extend empathy to themselves and, subsequently, to others.

Practicing self-compassion involves self-kindness, common humanity, and mindfulness. Self-kindness is the act of treating oneself with warmth and understanding, even in moments of failure or imperfection. It involves replacing self-criticism with self-encouragement and self- soothing. Recognizing one's common humanity is the acknowledgment that suffering and challenges are part of the human experience shared by all individuals. It helps individuals put their own struggles in perspective and reduce feelings of isolation. Mindfulness entails being aware of one's thoughts and emotions without judgment, allowing individuals to observe their inner experiences with curiosity and compassion.

A compassionate mindset extends beyond self-compassion to encompass compassion for others. This involves actively recognizing the suffering and needs of others and responding with empathy and support. Cultivating compassion for others requires developing empathy as a foundational skill. Empathy involves tuning into the emotions and perspectives of others, understanding their experiences, and responding with kindness and care. When individuals prioritize empathy and compassion in their interactions with others, they create a positive and supportive environment that fosters open communication as well as emotional connection.

One effective way to develop a compassionate mindset is through loving-kindness meditation, also known as metta meditation. Loving-kindness meditation is a mindfulness practice that entails sending well-wishes and loving intentions to oneself and others. It starts with directing these intentions toward oneself, gradually extending them to loved ones, acquaintances, and even individuals with whom one may have conflicts. By practicing loving-kindness meditation regularly, individuals can cultivate feelings of warmth, empathy, and compassion for themselves and others. This practice promotes a sense of interconnectedness and reinforces the idea that all beings deserve love and compassion.

Another approach to developing a compassionate mindset is through perspective-taking exercises. Perspective-taking encourages individuals to step into the shoes of others and imagine their emotions, thoughts, and experiences. It helps individuals understand different viewpoints and challenges their own biases and assumptions. Perspective-taking exercises can be as simple as reflecting on a situation from someone else's perspective or engaging in role-playing scenarios that require individuals to embody different roles and experiences. By regularly practicing perspective-taking, individuals can broaden their understanding of diverse perspectives and enhance their empathy and compassion.

Compassion-focused therapy (CFT) is a therapeutic strategy that focuses on developing self-compassion as well as compassion for others. CFT was developed by Dr. Paul Gilbert and is grounded in the idea that individuals can learn to be more compassionate by understanding the underlying processes of the mind. CFT involves exploring the evolutionary and psychological factors that influence self-criticism and self-compassion. Through CFT, individuals can develop self-soothing techniques and cultivate a compassionate inner voice. This therapy also emphasizes the importance of cultivating a compassionate mindset in daily life, leading to greater empathy and care for others.

Practicing acts of kindness and altruism is another effective way to foster a compassionate mindset. Acts of kindness involve intentional actions that benefit others, such as helping a friend in need, volunteering at a local charity, or offering support to a stranger. Compassion and empathy are practices that are reinforced when one performs acts of kindness for the benefit of others. It provides individuals with tangible experiences of the positive effect they can have on others' lives and deepens their sense of connection and caring.

Compassionate communication is a key aspect of developing a compassionate mindset. Compassionate communication involves listening to others with an open heart, acknowledging their feelings and needs, and responding with empathy and kindness. It requires setting aside judgment and defensiveness and creating a secure and supportive space for emotional expression. When individuals prioritize compassionate communication, they validate the emotions and experiences of others, fostering deeper connections and trust. Compassionate communication is essential in building empathy and nurturing compassionate relationships.

Mindful awareness is another essential element of a compassionate mindset. Mindful awareness entails being fully present in the moment and observing one's thoughts, emotions, and reactions with a non-judgmental attitude. It allows individuals to become more attuned to their own inner experiences and the experiences of others. By practicing mindful awareness, individuals can develop a greater capacity for empathy and compassion, as they become more skilled at recognizing and responding to the emotions and needs of themselves and those around them.

Educational programs and workshops that focus on empathy and compassion development can be highly beneficial in nurturing a compassionate mindset. These programs provide guidance, exercises, and opportunities for individuals to learn about the science of empathy and compassion and practice these skills in a structured setting. They often include activities that encourage perspective-taking, empathetic listening, and compassionate communication. By participating in these programs, individuals can deepen their understanding of empathy and compassion and apply them in their personal and social lives.

In conclusion, developing a compassionate mindset is a powerful way to enhance empathy and build more meaningful connections with others. Compassion begins with self-compassion, as individuals learn to treat themselves with kindness and understanding. It extends to compassion for others, as individuals practice empathy and actively respond to the suffering and needs of those around them. Cultivating a compassionate mindset involves practices such as self-compassion, loving-kindness meditation, perspective-taking, compassionate therapy, acts of kindness, compassionate communication, mindful awareness, and participation in empathy and compassion programs. By prioritizing compassion in daily life, individuals can contribute to a more empathetic and caring world, fostering positive relationships and a greater sense of interconnectedness with others. Developing a compassionate mindset is a journey of personal growth and transformation that leads to a deeper understanding of the human experience and a more compassionate and empathetic society.

Case Studies in Empathy

Empathy is a complex and multifaceted human ability that plays a pivotal role in our interactions with others. It involves comprehending and sharing the emotions and perspectives of others, fostering connection, compassion, and effective communication. Empathy is not a one-size-fits-all concept; it can manifest in various ways depending on individual experiences, circumstances, and the nature of the relationships involved. To gain a more profound understanding of how empathy operates in real-life situations, it is valuable to explore case studies that highlight its significance and impact. In this section, we will examine several case studies that illustrate the diverse expressions and consequences of empathy in different contexts.

Case Study 1: The Compassionate Healthcare Provider. In the healthcare field, empathy is a crucial component of patient care. A case study involves a nurse named Sarah who works in a busy hospital. One day, Sarah encounters a terminally ill patient, Emily, who is experiencing immense physical and emotional suffering. Instead of merely administering medications and treatments, Sarah takes the time to sit with Emily, listen to her fears and concerns, and offer a comforting presence. Through her empathy and compassion, Sarah not only alleviates Emily's distress but also strengthens their connection. Emily later expresses her gratitude for Sarah's support, emphasizing how her empathetic care made her feel seen and valued during her difficult journey. This case demonstrates the profound impact of empathy in healthcare, where it can improve the patient's emotional well-being and overall experience.

Case Study 2: The Empathetic Teacher. Empathy is also instrumental in the field of education. In this case study, we encounter a dedicated teacher, Mr. Anderson, who teaches a diverse group of high school students. One of his students, Maria, often struggles with schoolwork and appears disengaged. Rather than dismissing Maria's challenges, Mr. Anderson seeks to understand her perspective. Through open conversations and active listening, he learns that Maria faces significant family and personal issues that affect her academic performance. Mr. Anderson responds with empathy and adapts his teaching approach to provide additional support and encouragement to Maria. Over time, Maria's academic progress improves, and her attitude towards learning becomes more positive. This case highlights how empathy in education can empower students, foster trust between educators and students, and create a supportive learning environment.

Case Study 3: The Empathetic Leader. Empathy is a valuable trait for leaders in various settings. In this case study, we explore the story of a corporate executive, Alex, who leads a team of employees in a fast-paced organization. During a particularly challenging project, one of Alex's team members, Mark, is struggling to meet deadlines and appears overwhelmed. Instead of reprimanding Mark, Alex initiates a private conversation to inquire about his well-being and understand the reasons behind his difficulties. Mark opens up about personal stressors that have been affecting his performance. Alex responds with empathy by offering flexible work arrangements and connecting Mark with the company's employee assistance program. As a result, Mark's work improves, and his loyalty to the organization deepens. This case illustrates how empathy in leadership can enhance employee well-being, productivity, and overall team dynamics.

Case Study 4: The Empathetic Friend. Empathy is not limited to professional settings; it is equally essential in personal relationships. In this case study, we encounter two lifelong friends, Lisa and Sarah. Lisa is going through a challenging divorce and is overwhelmed by emotional turmoil. Sarah, recognizing Lisa's distress, consistently reaches out with empathy and support. She offers a nonjudgmental space for Lisa to express her feelings and shares stories of her own past struggles. Through their empathetic connection, Lisa feels less alone in her journey, and her emotional burden becomes more manageable. This case highlights the importance of empathy in friendships, where it can boost ties, offer consolation, and improve the emotional health of those going through a difficult period.

Case Study 5: The Empathetic Community. Empathy can extend beyond individual interactions to influence the dynamics of entire communities. In this case study, we explore a community that rallies together to support a family facing a tragedy. The Smith family experiences a devastating house fire, losing their home and belongings. In response, neighbors, friends, and community members mobilize to offer immediate assistance, shelter, and emotional support. This outpouring of empathy not only helps the Smiths during their time of crisis but also strengthens the sense of belonging and connectedness within the community. This case demonstrates how empathy can unite people, inspire collective action, and create resilient and compassionate communities.

Case Study 6: The Global Empathy Initiative. Empathy is not limited by cultural or geographic boundaries; it has the potential to address global issues and promote positive change. In this case study, we examine an international initiative aimed at addressing climate change and environmental sustainability. A wide range of organizations and activists work together to increase public awareness of the environmental issues the world is currently facing. They employ empathy as a driving force, emphasizing the interconnectedness of all living beings and the shared responsibility to protect the environment. Through their empathetic efforts, they mobilize individuals and governments to take meaningful action in addressing environmental issues. This case underscores the transformative power of empathy in addressing complex global challenges and promoting collective responsibility.

These case studies collectively illustrate the diverse ways in which empathy manifests and its far-reaching impact in various domains of life. Whether in healthcare, education, leadership, friendships, communities, or global initiatives, empathy serves as a catalyst for understanding, compassion, and positive change. Each case emphasizes that empathy is not a passive sentiment but an active force that enhances well-being, strengthens relationships, and contributes to a more empathetic and caring world.

In conclusion, empathy is a fundamental and multifaceted human trait that enriches our interactions with others and fosters meaningful connections. The case studies presented here showcase the diverse expressions and consequences of empathy in real-life situations. These stories highlight the transformative power of empathy in healthcare, education, leadership, friendships, communities, and global initiatives. They underscore the importance of empathy as a catalyst for understanding, compassion, and positive change. By recognizing the significance of empathy and actively cultivating it in our lives, we can contribute to a more empathetic and interconnected world where compassion and understanding thrive. Empathy serves as a reminder that, in the face of human complexity and diversity, our shared capacity for empathy can bridge gaps, build bridges, and ultimately make the world a more compassionate and empathetic place.

CHAPTER VII

Setting Boundaries

Importance of Boundaries

Boundaries are essential for maintaining healthy relationships, ensuring personal well-being, and establishing a sense of self. They serve as the invisible lines that define the limits of acceptable behavior, expectations, and interactions in various contexts, including personal relationships, professional environments, and social interactions. Boundaries act as a safeguard against harm, protect one's emotional and physical space, and contribute to a balanced and fulfilling life. In this section, we will explore the significance of boundaries, the different types of boundaries, and how to establish and maintain them effectively.

Boundaries in personal relationships are crucial for maintaining mutual respect and emotional well-being. These boundaries dictate the level of intimacy, trust, and vulnerability one is comfortable sharing with others. For example, individuals may establish boundaries around personal space, privacy, and emotional availability in a romantic relationship. By respecting these boundaries, both partners can maintain a sense of autonomy and mitigate the risk of conflicts and emotional burnout. Boundaries also help individuals clearly communicate their needs and preferences, fostering understanding and empathy between parties.

Professional boundaries are essential in the workplace to maintain a productive and respectful environment. These boundaries delineate appropriate behavior, expectations, and interactions between colleagues, supervisors, and subordinates. For instance, a manager should maintain professional boundaries by avoiding favoritism, refraining from sharing personal problems with employees, and respecting confidentiality. Professional boundaries contribute to a healthy work culture, reduce conflicts, and ensure that individuals are treated fairly and with dignity.

Emotional boundaries are essential for protecting one's emotional well-being and preventing emotional manipulation or harm. Emotional boundaries involve recognizing and communicating one's feelings, limits, and needs. For example, an individual may establish emotional boundaries by asserting their right to say "no" without guilt, setting limits on how much they can emotionally invest in a relationship, and identifying and expressing their emotional needs. By establishing and maintaining emotional boundaries, individuals can protect their mental health, prevent emotional exhaustion, and cultivate healthier relationships.

Physical boundaries encompass one's personal space and physical comfort. These boundaries can involve determining who can enter one's personal space, setting limits on physical touch, and establishing privacy preferences. In a healthcare setting, for instance, healthcare professionals must respect patients' physical boundaries by seeking consent for physical examinations and ensuring that patients feel comfortable and secure. Physical boundaries are crucial for ensuring safety and comfort and respecting individuals' autonomy over their bodies.

Social boundaries pertain to interactions within larger social groups and communities. They define the acceptable norms, values, and behaviors within a particular cultural or societal context. Social boundaries can manifest in various forms, such as taboos, etiquette, and cultural norms. For example, in some cultures, it may be considered impolite to engage in direct eye contact, while in others, it is a sign of respect. Understanding and respecting social boundaries are vital for effective communication and cultural competence.

Establishing and maintaining boundaries requires self-awareness, assertiveness, and effective communication skills. To establish boundaries, individuals must first identify their values, needs, and limits. Self-reflection can help individuals understand what is important to them and what they are willing to accept in their relationships and interactions. Once boundaries are established, it is essential to communicate them clearly and assertively to others. Open as well as honest communication is key to ensuring that others understand and respect these boundaries.

Setting boundaries also involves recognizing when they have been violated and taking appropriate action. When someone crosses a boundary, it is essential to assertively communicate the discomfort or violation and request that it not happen again. Boundaries are only effective when they are enforced consistently, and individuals should be prepared to take appropriate action if their boundaries continue to be disregarded.

The importance of boundaries extends to self-care and overall well-being. Without clear boundaries, individuals may find themselves overcommitted, emotionally drained, or constantly accommodating others' needs at the expense of their own. Boundaries act as a protective shield, allowing individuals to prioritize their mental and emotional health. Self-care involves setting boundaries around personal time, energy, and resources to ensure that individuals have the capacity to meet their own needs and engage in activities that promote well-being.

In conclusion, boundaries are a fundamental aspect of maintaining healthy relationships, preserving personal well-being, and fostering self-respect. They come in various forms, including personal, professional, emotional, physical, and social boundaries, and are crucial for defining acceptable behavior and interactions. Establishing and maintaining boundaries requires self- awareness, assertiveness, and effective communication skills. By recognizing the significance of boundaries and implementing them in various aspects of life, individuals can protect their emotional and physical well-being, maintain respectful relationships, and lead balanced and fulfilling lives. Boundaries are not a sign of selfishness but rather a vital tool for self-preservation and maintaining healthy connections with others.

Assertiveness Training

Setting and maintaining boundaries is an essential skill for healthy relationships, effective communication, and personal well-being. One of the most effective ways to establish and enforce boundaries is through assertiveness training. Assertiveness involves expressing one's needs, opinions, and limits in a clear, respectful, and confident manner while respecting the rights and boundaries of others. In this section, we will explore the importance of assertiveness training in setting boundaries, its key principles, and practical strategies for developing assertiveness skills.

Assertiveness is distinct from passivity and aggression, two communication styles that often hinder the establishment of healthy boundaries. Passivity involves yielding to others' demands and neglecting one's own needs and preferences. Passive individuals may find it challenging to assert their boundaries and may be prone to feeling overwhelmed or resentful. On the other hand, aggression involves disregarding others' rights and boundaries while forcefully imposing one's own needs and desires. Aggressive individuals may achieve short-term compliance but damage relationships and create conflict in the long run. Assertiveness strikes a balance between these two extremes, allowing individuals to express themselves confidently and respectfully while considering the needs and boundaries of others.

One of the fundamental principles of assertiveness training is self-awareness. Before individuals can effectively communicate their boundaries, they must first identify their values, needs, and limits. Self-reflection and introspection are essential tools in this process. Understanding what is personally important and recognizing when a boundary has been crossed are critical components of assertive communication. For instance, someone in a romantic relationship may realize that they need more personal space and alone time to recharge. Acknowledging this need is the first step toward setting boundaries that protect their emotional well-being.

Self-esteem is closely linked to assertiveness. Individuals with healthy self-esteem will likely assert their boundaries confidently and believe that their needs and opinions are valid. Low self-esteem can undermine assertiveness, leading individuals to doubt their worth and hesitate in expressing their boundaries. Building self-esteem involves challenging negative self-talk, setting achievable goals, and practicing self-compassion. The more individuals value themselves, the more they are willing to assert their boundaries and protect their well-being.

Effective communication is a cornerstone of assertiveness. When setting boundaries, it is crucial to express oneself clearly, directly, and respectfully. Using "I" statements is an effective technique in assertive communication. For example, saying, "I feel overwhelmed when you ask me to take on additional tasks at work" conveys one's emotions and concerns without blaming or accusing. Additionally, active listening is a crucial element of assertive communication. It involves genuinely hearing and understanding the perspectives of others, which can help individuals address potential conflicts and reach mutually beneficial solutions.

Boundary setting often involves saying "no" when necessary. Many people find saying "no" challenging due to fear of rejection or conflict. Assertiveness training teaches individuals how to say "no" in a polite and firm manner. For example, instead of saying "I can't do that," which may leave room for negotiation, an assertive response might be, "I appreciate the opportunity, but I'm unable to take on additional commitments right now." This communicates the refusal clearly and respectfully while maintaining one's boundaries.

Learning to handle criticism and pushback is another crucial aspect of assertiveness training. When individuals assert their boundaries, they may encounter resistance or criticism from others who do not respect those boundaries. In such situations, it is important to remain calm and composed while respectfully reinforcing one's boundaries. For instance, if a coworker criticizes a boundary set at work, an assertive response could be, "I understand your perspective, but I need to maintain this boundary for my well-being."

Conflict resolution is an inherent part of boundary setting. Assertiveness training equips individuals with conflict resolution skills that help address disagreements and conflicts constructively. The focus shifts from winning or losing to finding mutually beneficial solutions. Individuals learn how to express their needs, listen actively to others, and collaborate to reach resolutions that respect everyone's boundaries. Conflict resolution skills are valuable in personal and professional relationships, as they prevent conflicts from escalating and foster a culture of open communication.

Developing assertiveness skills requires practice and reinforcement. Role-playing exercises, assertiveness workshops, and therapy can be helpful in building and strengthening assertive communication skills. Role-playing allows individuals to simulate real-life scenarios and practice assertive responses in a safe and supportive environment. Assertiveness workshops provide structured training and guidance, while therapy can help individuals explore underlying issues that may be hindering their assertiveness.

The benefits of assertiveness training in setting boundaries extend to various aspects of life. In personal relationships, assertiveness helps individuals establish clear expectations and communicate their needs and limits, reducing misunderstandings and conflicts. In the workplace, assertiveness enhances communication, teamwork, and professional growth. It allows employees to advocate for themselves, negotiate effectively, and maintain a healthy work-life balance. In social interactions, assertiveness fosters genuine connections, as individuals can express themselves authentically and maintain boundaries that promote well-being.
One of the most significant advantages of assertiveness training is its positive influence on mental health. By asserting boundaries and expressing oneself assertively, individuals reduce stress, anxiety, and resentment. They also enhance their self-esteem and self-confidence, leading to improved overall well-being. Assertiveness allows individuals to prioritize their mental and emotional health, protecting themselves from burnout and emotional exhaustion.

In conclusion, assertiveness training is a powerful tool for setting and maintaining healthy boundaries. It empowers individuals to express their needs, opinions, and limits confidently and respectfully while considering the rights and boundaries of others. Assertiveness training involves principles such as self-awareness, self-esteem, effective communication, active listening, saying "no" when necessary, handling criticism, conflict resolution, and continuous practice. By mastering assertiveness skills, individuals can build and maintain healthy relationships, achieve personal and professional success, and protect their mental and emotional well-being. Assertiveness is a valuable skill that contributes to a balanced and a fulfilling life, allowing individuals to live authentically and in alignment with their values and boundaries.

Maintaining Healthy Limits

Setting boundaries is a crucial aspect of interpersonal relationships, self-care, and overall well-being. However, it is equally essential to maintain healthy limits when establishing these boundaries. Healthy limits refer to the balance between asserting one's needs, values, and boundaries while respecting the autonomy and boundaries of others. Striking this balance is crucial for fostering healthy relationships, preventing conflicts, and ensuring that boundaries serve their intended purpose. In this section, we will explore the significance of maintaining healthy limits in setting boundaries, the challenges that may arise, and strategies for achieving this delicate equilibrium.

Boundaries are not static; they are flexible and context-dependent. Maintaining healthy limits means recognizing that boundaries may need to adapt to different situations and individuals. For example, the boundaries one sets with a romantic partner may differ from those with a coworker or a friend. Understanding that boundaries can vary depending on the context and the people involved is crucial for effective boundary maintenance.

One challenge in maintaining healthy limits is finding the balance between being too rigid and too accommodating. Overly rigid boundaries can result in isolation and difficulty forming meaningful connections with others. On the other hand, being overly accommodating or having weak boundaries can result in feeling overwhelmed, exploited, or drained by constantly meeting others' needs at the expense of one's own. Achieving a healthy balance involves being firm in asserting one's boundaries when necessary while remaining open to negotiation and flexibility when appropriate.

Effective communication is pivotal in maintaining healthy limits. It is essential to communicate boundaries clearly, assertively, and respectfully. However, it is equally important to listen actively and empathetically when others express their boundaries. When individuals communicate their boundaries, they should be receptive to feedback and also willing to participate in a constructive dialogue. Healthy limits encompass both expressing oneself authentically and valuing the perspectives and boundaries of others.

Maintaining healthy limits also requires recognizing when boundaries have been crossed and taking appropriate action. When someone violates a boundary, it is crucial to assertively communicate the discomfort or violation and request that it not happen again. However, individuals should be prepared to enforce their boundaries consistently if they continue to be disregarded. This may involve setting consequences or, in extreme cases, reevaluating the relationship.

In maintaining healthy limits, it is essential to differentiate between assertiveness and aggression. Being assertive involves expressing one's needs and boundaries in a respectful and confident manner while respecting the rights and boundaries of others. Aggression, on the other hand, involves forcefully imposing one's needs and desires without regard for others. Striking the right balance between assertiveness and aggression ensures that boundaries are maintained without causing harm or conflict.

Cultural and societal norms can influence the boundaries individuals establish and maintain. Cultural differences in personal space, communication styles, and expectations can lead to misunderstandings or conflicts when interacting with individuals from diverse backgrounds. Maintaining healthy limits in a multicultural context requires cultural sensitivity, open-mindedness, and a willingness to adapt one's boundaries to accommodate cultural differences when appropriate.

Self-care is an integral component of maintaining healthy limits. Recognizing and prioritizing one's physical, emotional, and mental well-being is essential for setting and enforcing boundaries effectively. Self-care involves setting boundaries around personal time, energy, and resources to ensure that individuals have the capacity to meet their own needs and engage in activities that promote well-being. Neglecting self-care can lead to resentment, burnout, and difficulty maintaining boundaries.

Boundaries within intimate relationships often present unique challenges. Couples may grapple with issues related to personal space, emotional intimacy, and autonomy. Maintaining healthy limits in romantic relationships involves mutual respect, open communication, and a willingness to negotiate and compromise. Couples should engage in regular discussions about their boundaries, reassess them as needed, and be sensitive to each other's changing needs and circumstances.

In the workplace, maintaining healthy limits is essential for professional well-being and effective teamwork. Employees should assert their boundaries regarding workload, work hours, and personal space while respecting the boundaries of their colleagues and supervisors. Employers, in turn, should promote a healthy work-life balance, respect employees' boundaries, and provide support for managing stress and workload.

Family dynamics can also present unique challenges in maintaining healthy limits. Family members may have longstanding patterns of behavior and expectations that can make boundary setting more complex. Effective communication, therapy, and family discussions can help address boundary issues within families and foster healthier relationships.

Maintaining healthy limits extends beyond individual relationships and encompasses broader social and cultural contexts. Society's norms and expectations can influence the boundaries individuals set and maintain in various areas of life, including gender roles, personal space, and privacy. Challenging societal norms that perpetuate unhealthy boundaries or discrimination is a collective effort that can lead to positive social change.

In conclusion, maintaining healthy limits in setting boundaries is crucial for fostering healthy relationships, preventing conflicts, and ensuring that boundaries serve their intended purpose. Healthy limits involve finding a balance between asserting one's needs and respecting the autonomy and boundaries of others. Challenges in maintaining healthy limits include balancing rigidity and accommodation, effective communication, recognizing boundary violations, differentiating between assertiveness and aggression, cultural sensitivity, self-care, and addressing boundary issues in intimate relationships, the workplace, and within families. By mastering the art of maintaining healthy limits, individuals can protect their well-being, build meaningful connections with others, and lead balanced and fulfilling lives. Healthy boundaries are not a sign of selfishness but rather a cornerstone of healthy relationships and individual well-being.

CHAPTER VIII

Forgiveness and Reconciliation

The Power of Forgiveness

Forgiveness is a profound and transformative human experience that holds the potential to heal emotional wounds, mend broken relationships, and free individuals from the burden of resentment and anger. It is letting go of past grievances and releasing negative emotions and thoughts associated with a hurtful event or person. Forgiveness is a complex and multifaceted process, and its power lies in its ability to bring about inner peace, promote emotional well-being, and foster reconciliation. In this section, we will explore the significance of forgiveness, its psychological and emotional benefits, its challenges, and practical strategies for embracing the power of forgiveness in our lives.

Forgiveness is often misunderstood as condoning or excusing harmful behavior. However, it is essential to recognize that forgiveness is not about absolving the wrongdoer of responsibility or endorsing their actions. Instead, it is a deeply personal choice to release the grip of anger, resentment, and negative emotions that bind the victim to the hurtful event or person. Forgiveness empowers individuals to take control of their emotional well-being and transcend the pain and suffering caused by the wrongdoing.

The psychological and emotional benefits of forgiveness are significant. Research in psychology has shown that forgiving others can lead to reduced stress, anxiety, as well as depression. It can also enhance self-esteem and self-worth by freeing individuals from the emotional weight of grudges and grievances. Forgiveness promotes emotional resilience, allowing individuals to bounce back from adversity and find meaning and purpose in their lives. Moreover, forgiving others can improve the quality of relationships and lead to greater life satisfaction and overall well-being.

Forgiveness has a profound impact on personal relationships. It has the power to mend fractured bonds and restore trust and intimacy. In cases of conflicts or betrayals within families, friendships, or romantic relationships, forgiveness can pave the way for reconciliation and healing. It allows individuals to move beyond the hurtful event and rebuild connections based on empathy, understanding, and compassion. Forgiving others is a courageous act that requires vulnerability and a willingness to let go of the need for vengeance or retribution.

The process of forgiveness is not without its challenges. Forgiving someone who has caused pain or harm can be incredibly difficult, and it may take time to work through the emotions and thoughts associated with the hurtful event. One common obstacle to forgiveness is the belief that it implies weakness or capitulation. Some individuals may resist forgiveness because they fear it will diminish their sense of justice or validate the wrongdoer's actions. However, forgiveness is not synonymous with weakness; it is a courageous act of choosing peace and emotional liberation over continued suffering.

Another challenge in the forgiveness process is the misconception that forgiveness requires reconciliation with the wrongdoer. While forgiveness can pave the way for reconciliation, it is not a prerequisite. Sometimes, reconciliation may not be possible or advisable due to the offense's nature or the victim's safety. Forgiveness can occur independently, allowing individuals to find closure and inner peace without necessarily resuming a relationship with the wrongdoer.

The fear of being hurt again may also hinder forgiveness. Individuals who have experienced betrayal or harm in the past may worry that forgiving the wrongdoer will make them vulnerable to further mistreatment. However, forgiveness does not require individuals to place themselves in harm's way or trust those who have repeatedly shown themselves to be untrustworthy. Setting healthy boundaries and protecting oneself from further harm is compatible with the forgiveness process.

Practical strategies can help individuals embrace the power of forgiveness in their lives. One approach is to cultivate empathy and understanding by considering the perspective and circumstances of the wrongdoer. This does not excuse their actions but can provide insight into the factors that may have contributed to their behavior. Understanding that individuals who hurt others often carry their own emotional baggage and wounds can foster compassion and facilitate forgiveness.

Journaling is another effective tool for processing and releasing negative emotions associated with a hurtful event. Writing down one's thoughts, feelings, and experiences related to the offense can help individuals gain clarity and perspective. Journaling can also serve as a means of self-reflection and self-compassion, allowing individuals to acknowledge their pain and gradually release it through the written word.

Seeking support from trusted friends, family members, or mental health professionals can be invaluable in the forgiveness process. Sharing one's feelings and experiences with a supportive and empathetic listener can provide validation and encouragement. Professional guidance can offer specific techniques and strategies tailored to the individual's unique circumstances and challenges.

Ultimately, forgiveness is a choice—an act of self-empowerment and emotional liberation. It is not a one-size-fits-all process, and the timeline for forgiveness varies from person to person and situation to situation. Some wounds may require more time and effort to heal than others. It is imperative to exercise patience and compassion towards oneself when embarking on the process of forgiveness.

In conclusion, forgiveness is a strong and life-changing human experience that has the capacity to mend relationships, heal emotional wounds, and foster inner peace and wellbeing. It is not about condoning or excusing harmful behavior but about releasing the grip of anger, resentment, and negative emotions that bind individuals to past grievances. Forgiveness offers psychological and emotional benefits, including reduced stress and enhanced self-esteem, and can improve the quality of personal relationships. While forgiveness poses challenges, such as misconceptions about weakness or the fear of being hurt again, practical strategies and support can help individuals embrace the power of forgiveness in their lives. Forgiveness is a courageous act of choosing peace, healing, and emotional liberation over continued suffering, and it has the potential to transform lives and relationships for the better.

Steps Toward Reconciliation

Reconciliation is a profound and challenging process of healing as well as rebuilding trust in the aftermath of conflict, hurtful events, or strained relationships. It involves a deliberate and mutual effort to repair emotional and relational damage and move toward a renewed sense of understanding, empathy, and connection. Reconciliation is not always possible or appropriate in every situation, and it requires commitment, patience, and open communication from all parties involved. In this section, we will explore the significance of reconciliation, the steps toward achieving it, the obstacles that may arise, and the potential rewards of this transformative journey.

The significance of reconciliation lies in its potential to mend broken bonds and promote healing, forgiveness, and emotional well-being. It allows individuals or groups to move beyond the pain and anger caused by conflicts or hurtful events and rebuild relationships based on trust, understanding, and mutual respect. Reconciliation is a powerful process that can bring closure to unresolved issues, foster personal growth, and create a sense of unity and harmony.

One of the initial steps toward reconciliation is acknowledging the pain and hurt that have occurred. This involves a willingness to confront the emotions and experiences associated with the conflict or harm. Acknowledgment is an essential foundation for reconciliation because it validates the experiences of those who have been hurt and opens the door to understanding the impact of one's actions or decisions on others. It requires individuals or parties to take responsibility for their role in the conflict or harm and express remorse or empathy.

Effective communication is paramount in the reconciliation process. Open and honest dialogue allows individuals or groups to express their feelings, concerns, and needs, as well as to listen actively to the perspectives of others. Communication involves active listening, empathy, and a willingness to consider alternative viewpoints. Through this process, misunderstandings can be clarified, grievances can be addressed, and common ground can be found.

Forgiveness is a critical component of reconciliation. It is letting go of past grievances and releasing negative emotions and thoughts associated with the conflict or harm. Forgiveness does not mean condoning or excusing the wrongdoing; rather, it is a personal choice to free oneself from the emotional burden of anger and resentment. Forgiveness permits individuals to heal and move forward with a sense of peace and emotional liberation.

Rebuilding trust is often a challenging and time-consuming aspect of reconciliation. Trust may have been damaged or eroded during the conflict or harm, and regaining it requires consistent actions and behaviors that shows reliability and sincerity. Rebuilding trust involves keeping promises, being transparent, and demonstrating a commitment to change and growth. It also involves recognizing that trust may be rebuilt gradually and that setbacks or doubts may arise along the way.

Restitution or reparations may be necessary in cases where tangible harm or damage has occurred. This step involves taking concrete actions to rectify the harm done and address the consequences of one's actions. For example, in cases of financial harm or property damage, restitution may involve compensating the affected party. Restitution is a tangible way to demonstrate accountability and commitment to making amends. Reconciliation may sometimes require mediation or facilitated dialogues, especially when conflicts involve multiple parties or deep-rooted issues. Mediation entails a neutral third party who facilitates communication and negotiation between the parties involved. It can help create a safe and structured environment for productive discussions and problem-solving. Facilitated dialogues aim to promote understanding, empathy, and resolution through guided conversations.

While reconciliation offers the potential for healing and growth, it is not always possible or appropriate in every situation. Some conflicts may be irreparable, and individuals or parties may be unwilling or unable to engage in the reconciliation process. Additionally, safety concerns must always be considered; reconciliation should never compromise the safety or well-being of individuals involved.

Obstacles to reconciliation can include entrenched resentment, unwillingness to communicate or compromise, unresolved power imbalances, or the absence of remorse or accountability. These obstacles can hinder progress and require additional effort, patience, and support to overcome. In cases where reconciliation seems unattainable, individuals may need to focus on personal healing and finding closure independently.

The rewards of reconciliation can be profound and far-reaching. Reconciliation can bring closure to unresolved conflicts, promote emotional healing, and enhance personal growth and self-awareness. It can lead to stronger as well as more meaningful relationships based on trust, empathy, and mutual respect. Additionally, reconciliation can have a positive ripple effect, fostering peace and harmony within families, communities, and societies.

In conclusion, reconciliation is a transformative process that holds the potential to heal emotional wounds, mend broken relationships, and promote understanding and empathy. It involves acknowledging pain, effective communication, forgiveness, rebuilding trust, and sometimes restitution or mediation. While reconciliation is not always possible or appropriate, it offers the opportunity for healing, growth, and renewed connection. It requires patience, commitment, as well as a willingness to confront obstacles and challenges along the way. Ultimately, reconciliation can bring about closure, foster personal well-being, and contribute to a more harmonious and compassionate world.

Stories of Healing

Throughout history, human beings have demonstrated incredible resilience and the capacity for healing in the face of adversity, trauma, and pain. Stories of healing are a testament to the strength of the human spirit and sources of inspiration and hope for those facing their own challenges. These narratives reveal individuals' various paths to overcome physical and emotional wounds, find meaning in their experiences, and emerge from darkness into the light of recovery. In this section, we will explore the significance of stories of healing, the common themes and lessons they offer, and the role they play in fostering empathy, understanding, and connection among individuals and communities.

The significance of stories of healing lies in their power to inspire and uplift. These narratives demonstrate that healing is possible, even in the most challenging circumstances. They provide a sense of hope for those who may be struggling with their own wounds, offering a glimpse into the potential for transformation and recovery. Healing stories also remind that human beings possess an innate resilience that enables them to adapt, grow, and find meaning in their experiences.

One common theme in stories of healing is the journey from suffering to resilience. Many individuals who have experienced trauma or adversity initially grapple with overwhelming pain, grief, or despair. However, as they embark on their healing journey, they gradually develop coping mechanisms, seek support, and find ways to navigate their emotions. This transformation from suffering to resilience illustrates the human capacity to overcome hardship and emerge stronger on the other side.

Empathy is another key element in stories of healing. When individuals share their healing journeys, they invite others to walk in their shoes and experience their pain, challenges, and triumphs. This sharing of experiences fosters empathy, compassion, and a deeper understanding of the human condition. Readers or listeners of these stories are more likely to connect with and support those facing similar challenges, as they gain insight into the emotional complexities of healing.

The process of finding meaning in adversity is a recurrent theme in stories of healing. Individuals often reflect on their experiences, searching for a sense of purpose or a deeper understanding of themselves and the world around them. This search for meaning can lead to personal growth, resilience, and renewed sense of purpose. Many individuals who have faced adversity emerge from their healing journey with a profound appreciation for life and a desire to positively impact others.

Forgiveness is a powerful theme in many stories of healing. Individuals who have experienced harm or betrayal often grapple with anger, resentment, and the desire for revenge. However, as they progress on their healing journey, some choose to forgive those who have caused them pain. Forgiveness is about letting go of the emotional weight of bitterness and anger, not about endorsing or justifying bad behavior. It is a liberating act that allows individuals to move forward with a sense of peace and emotional liberation.

The role of support and community in healing stories is evident. Many individuals credit their healing journeys to the presence of supportive friends, family members, therapists, or communities. Having a strong support system can make a significant difference in the healing process, providing a sense of validation, encouragement, and connection. Supportive relationships often play a crucial role in helping individuals navigate their emotions, seek professional help when needed, and find the strength to persevere.

Resilience is a recurring theme in stories of healing. Resilience is known as the capability to bounce back from adversity, adapt to challenges, and thrive despite difficult circumstances. Individuals who share their healing stories often highlight the resilience they have developed through their experiences. They emphasize the importance of embracing adversity as an opportunity for growth and transformation. Resilience is not an innate trait but it is a skill that can be cultivated and strengthened through healing.

Transformation is a central element in stories of healing. Individuals who have experienced trauma or adversity often undergo profound personal transformations. They may develop a deeper sense of self-awareness, empathy, and purpose. Their perspectives on life, relationships, and the world may shift, leading to a greater appreciation for the beauty and fragility of human existence. These transformations illustrate the potential for growth and positive change that can emerge from healing journeys.

The role of storytelling in healing is fundamental. Sharing one's healing journey through storytelling serves several purposes. It allows individuals to process their experiences, gain clarity and perspective, and find a sense of closure. Additionally, storytelling can inspire and uplift others who may be facing similar challenges. It offers a sense of hope and a reminder that healing is possible. Moreover, storytelling fosters connection and empathy among individuals and communities, as it invites others to engage with and support those who have experienced trauma or adversity.

In conclusion, stories of healing are powerful narratives that showcase the human capacity for resilience, transformation, and empathy. They provide hope and inspiration for those facing their own challenges and offer insight into the healing journey from suffering to resilience. Common themes in these stories include the search for meaning in adversity, the role of support and community, the power of forgiveness, and the significance of personal transformation. Through storytelling, individuals can process their experiences, connect with others, and contribute to a deeper understanding of the human condition. Stories of healing remind us that, even in the face of adversity, the human spirit has the potential to shine brightly and emerge from darkness into the light of recovery.

CHAPTER IX

Dealing with Specific Types of Difficult Individuals

Narcissists

Navigating relationships with difficult individuals can be challenging, but dealing with narcissists presents a unique set of complexities and obstacles. Narcissistic individuals exhibit traits such as grandiosity, entitlement, a lack of empathy, and an overwhelming demand for admiration and attention. These characteristics can make interactions with them particularly challenging and often result in conflicts, manipulation, and emotional turmoil for those involved. In this section, we will explore the dynamics of dealing with narcissists, strategies for effective communication, and the significance of setting boundaries to protect one's well-being.

Narcissistic individuals often display a sense of superiority and entitlement, which can lead to difficulties in communication. They may belittle others, dismiss their opinions, or dominate conversations. In such interactions, it is essential to maintain assertiveness and self-confidence while avoiding confrontation or power struggles. One effective communication strategy is to stay calm, express one's thoughts and feelings clearly, and avoid reacting emotionally to provocations. By staying composed and assertive, individuals can maintain their own sense of self-worth and minimize the narcissist's attempts to control the conversation.

Narcissists thrive on attention and admiration, making them skilled manipulators who often seek to exploit others for their own gain. They may use tactics such as gaslighting, guilt-tripping, or emotional manipulation to control and manipulate those around them. Recognizing these tactics is crucial in dealing with narcissists. Individuals must trust their instincts and validate their feelings rather than falling into the narcissist's web of manipulation. Seeking support from trusted friends, family members, or professionals can provide validation and guidance when dealing with manipulative behavior.

Setting boundaries is essential when dealing with narcissists. Narcissistic individuals may disregard personal boundaries and invade the space and privacy of others. Establishing and enforcing clear boundaries is crucial for maintaining one's emotional and psychological well-being. Communicating boundaries assertively and consistently is essential, using "I" statements to express one's needs and limits. While narcissists may resist or challenge boundaries, it is crucial to stand firm and prioritize self-care.

Empathy is often lacking in narcissistic individuals, as they struggle to understand or link to the emotions as well as experiences of others. When dealing with narcissists, it is vital to manage expectations regarding their capacity for empathy. Individuals should be prepared for limited understanding and be cautious about sharing vulnerable or personal information. Instead, focus on clear and direct communication, as narcissists may respond better to logical arguments rather than appeals to emotions.

Maintaining one's self-esteem and self-worth is challenging when dealing with narcissists, as they may employ tactics to undermine others' confidence and self-esteem. To counteract this, individuals must cultivate a strong sense of self-esteem independently of the narcissist's opinions or criticisms. Self-affirmation, positive self-talk, and seeking validation from trusted sources can help individuals maintain their self-worth and resist the negative impact of narcissistic behavior.

It is essential to recognize that changing a narcissist's behavior is a challenging and often fruitless endeavor. Narcissistic traits are deeply ingrained, and individuals with narcissistic personality disorder may resist or deny any need for change. While it is possible for some narcissists to seek therapy and make progress, this change typically requires self-awareness and a genuine desire to change, which are often lacking in narcissistic individuals. Therefore, those dealing with narcissists must focus on managing their own responses and boundaries rather than trying to change the narcissist.

In some cases, maintaining distance or limiting contact with narcissists may be the most effective strategy for self-preservation. Narcissistic individuals can be emotionally draining and damaging to those around them. Suppose interactions with a narcissist consistently lead to emotional distress or conflict. In that case, it may be necessary to reevaluate the level of contact and establish stricter boundaries, including potentially cutting ties altogether if the situation warrants it.

Support and self-care are vital when dealing with narcissists. It can be emotionally taxing to engage with individuals who exhibit narcissistic traits, and seeking support from friends, family, or professionals can provide validation, guidance, and a sense of perspective. Engaging in self-care practices such as mindfulness, relaxation techniques, and therapy can help individuals manage the stress and emotional toll of dealing with narcissists.

In conclusion, dealing with narcissists presents a unique set of challenges due to their grandiosity, manipulation, lack of empathy, and need for admiration. Effective communication strategies involve maintaining assertiveness, recognizing manipulative tactics, setting clear boundaries, and managing expectations regarding empathy. It is crucial to prioritize self-esteem, self-worth, and self-care when dealing with narcissists, as their behavior can be emotionally draining and damaging. While changing a narcissist's behavior is typically challenging, individuals can focus on managing their own responses and boundaries to protect their well-being. In some cases, maintaining distance or limiting contact may be necessary for self-preservation. Dealing with narcissists requires resilience, self-awareness, and a commitment to protecting one's emotional and psychological well-being.

Manipulators

Having to deal with manipulators can be difficult and emotionally draining. Manipulative individuals often use cunning tactics to control or exploit others for their own gain, leaving their victims feeling confused, frustrated, and emotionally drained. Manipulation can manifest in various forms, from subtle emotional manipulation to overt deception and coercion. This section will explore the dynamics of dealing with manipulators, strategies for recognizing manipulation, and approaches for protecting one's well-being and autonomy.

Manipulators often rely on emotional manipulation to control their victims. They may use guilt-tripping, shaming, or playing the victim to induce feelings of guilt or obligation in others. Recognizing emotional manipulation requires a keen awareness of one's emotions and boundaries. Valuing one's feelings and questioning any attempts to manipulate or undermine them is essential. Setting and maintaining clear boundaries is crucial in dealing with emotional manipulation, as manipulators may disregard personal limits and invade emotional space.

Gaslighting is a specifically insidious form of manipulation in which the manipulator seeks to undermine the victim's sense of reality or sanity. Gaslighting may involve denying past conversations, events, or promises, causing the victim to doubt their own memory or perception. To combat gaslighting, individuals must trust their own memory and judgment. Keeping a journal or written record of important conversations and events can provide evidence when faced with gaslighting attempts. Seeking help from trusted family members or friends can also help validate one's experiences and provide an external perspective.

Deception and lying are common tactics employed by manipulators to achieve their goals. Manipulative individuals may tell half-truths, withhold information, or outright lie to manipulate others into compliance. Recognizing deception requires careful scrutiny of the information being presented and an awareness of inconsistencies or discrepancies. When dealing with manipulators, it is crucial to ask questions, seek clarification, and verify information. Trust should be earned through consistent honesty rather than granted automatically.

Manipulators may exploit vulnerability and empathy by using pity or sympathy to gain an advantage. They may exaggerate their hardships or portray themselves as victims needing help or support. Recognizing this form of manipulation involves assessing the consistency and credibility of the manipulator's claims. It is essential to keep a healthy level of skepticism and avoid rushing to the aid of someone who may be exploiting one's compassion. Asking for evidence or validation of their claims can help determine the authenticity of the manipulator's story.

Coercion and pressure are tactics manipulators use to force others into compliance. They may employ threats, intimidation, or ultimatums to manipulate individuals into doing what they want. Dealing with coercive manipulation requires a firm commitment to one's principles and values. Individuals must assert their boundaries and communicate their refusal to engage in actions that go against their beliefs or interests. It is essential to recognize that compliance under duress is not consent, and individuals have the right to protect their autonomy.

Manipulative individuals may also employ flattery or charm to manipulate and gain favor with others. While compliments and positive feedback are normal in social interactions, excessive flattery or insincere charm should be met with caution. Recognizing manipulative charm involves assessing whether the flattery serves a particular agenda or whether it is consistent with the individual's overall behavior and intentions. Maintaining a healthy level of skepticism and questioning excessive flattery can help individuals avoid falling prey to manipulative tactics.

Maintaining one's self-esteem and self-worth is vital when dealing with manipulators, as they may employ tactics to undermine others' confidence and self-esteem. Manipulators may criticize, belittle, or devalue their victims to exert control or gain an advantage. To counteract this, individuals must cultivate a strong sense of self-esteem independently of the manipulator's opinions or criticisms. Self-affirmation, positive self-talk, and seeking validation from trusted sources can help individuals maintain their self-worth and resist the negative impact of manipulative behavior.

Setting and enforcing boundaries is a critical aspect of dealing with manipulators. Manipulative individuals often disregard personal boundaries and invade the emotional or physical space of others. Establishing clear boundaries and communicating them assertively is crucial for protecting one's autonomy and well-being. It is essential to express one's limits and expectations clearly and consistently and to enforce consequences when boundaries are violated.

In some cases, maintaining distance or limiting contact with manipulators may be the most effective strategy for self-preservation. Manipulative individuals can be emotionally draining and damaging to those around them. Suppose interactions with a manipulator consistently lead to emotional distress or conflict. In that case, it may be necessary to reevaluate the level of contact and establish stricter boundaries, including potentially cutting ties altogether if the situation warrants it.

Support and self-care are vital when dealing with manipulators. It can be emotionally taxing to engage with individuals who employ manipulative tactics, and seeking support from friends, family, or professionals can provide validation, guidance, and a sense of perspective. Engaging in self-care practices such as mindfulness, relaxation techniques, and therapy can help individuals manage the stress and emotional toll of dealing with manipulators.

In conclusion, dealing with manipulators requires a combination of awareness, assertiveness, and self-care. Recognizing manipulation tactics such as emotional manipulation, gaslighting, deception, exploitation of vulnerability, coercion, and charm is essential for protecting one's well-being and autonomy. Maintaining self-esteem and self-worth independently of the manipulator's opinions is crucial. Setting and enforcing clear boundaries, along with the possibility of limiting contact, can help individuals protect their autonomy and emotional health. Seeking support and practicing self-care are vital in managing the emotional toll of dealing with manipulators. Ultimately, individuals must prioritize their well-being and protect themselves from the manipulative tactics of others.

Aggressive Personalities

Dealing with aggressive personalities can be a challenging and emotionally taxing experience. Aggressive individuals often exhibit hostile, confrontational, or intimidating behaviors that can lead to conflicts, stress, and emotional distress for those involved. Aggression can manifest in various forms, from verbal and physical aggression to passive-aggressive behavior. In this section, we will explore the dynamics of dealing with aggressive personalities, strategies for recognizing aggression, and approaches for protecting one's well-being and fostering effective communication.

Aggressive individuals may resort to verbal aggression, using insults, threats, or offensive language to assert dominance or control. Recognizing verbal aggression involves acknowledging the disrespectful or demeaning nature of the communication. It is essential to remain composed and refrain from reacting emotionally to verbal attacks. Responding assertively rather than defensively can help maintain one's self-esteem and set a boundary against further aggression.

Physical aggression is a more direct and immediate form of hostility. Aggressive individuals may resort to physical violence, threats, or intimidation to assert their dominance or control over others. When faced with physical aggression, it is crucial to prioritize security and seek immediate assistance from authorities or support networks. Physical aggression should never be tolerated, and individuals have the right to protect themselves and ensure their safety.

Passive-aggressive behavior is a less overt but equally harmful form of aggression. Passive-aggressive individuals may express hostility indirectly, through sarcasm, sulking, or withholding cooperation. Recognizing passive-aggressive behavior requires attentiveness to subtle signs of resistance or uncooperativeness. Addressing passive-aggressive behavior directly and assertively is essential, seeking clarity and open communication to resolve underlying issues.

Manipulation and control are common motives behind aggression. Aggressive individuals may use confrontational or intimidating tactics to achieve their goals or maintain power and control over others. Recognizing manipulation and control involves assessing whether the aggressive behavior aims to exert dominance or achieve specific outcomes. When faced with manipulative aggression, it is crucial to assert one's autonomy and protect personal boundaries.

Conflict resolution strategies are essential when dealing with aggressive personalities. Effective communication and conflict resolution techniques can help de-escalate confrontations and foster understanding. Active listening, empathy, and assertive communication are valuable tools for diffusing tension and promoting productive dialogue. Individuals should focus on addressing the underlying issues rather than engaging in power struggles or retaliatory aggression.

Maintaining one's composure and emotional control is vital when dealing with aggressive individuals. Aggressive behavior often aims to provoke emotional reactions in others. It is essential to resist the urge to react impulsively or emotionally to provocation. Instead, individuals should strive to remain calm and composed, responding assertively and rationally to confrontational situations.

Setting boundaries is crucial when dealing with aggressive personalities. Aggressive individuals may disregard personal boundaries and invade the emotional or physical space of others. Establishing clear boundaries and communicating them assertively is essential for protecting one's autonomy and well-being. Individuals should express their limits and expectations clearly and consistently and be prepared to enforce consequences when boundaries are violated.

Avoiding escalation is a primary goal when dealing with aggressive personalities. Engaging in power struggles or retaliatory aggression can exacerbate conflicts and lead to further hostility. Choosing one's battles wisely and prioritizing conflict resolution over confrontation is essential. Individuals should seek opportunities for de-escalation and conflict resolution rather than escalating conflicts through aggression.

Seeking support and self-care are vital when dealing with aggressive individuals. It can be emotionally taxing to engage with individuals who exhibit aggressive behaviors, and seeking support from friends, family, or professionals can provide validation, guidance, and a sense of perspective. Engaging in self-care practices such as mindfulness, relaxation techniques, and therapy can help individuals manage the stress and emotional toll of dealing with aggression.

In some cases, maintaining distance or limiting contact with aggressive individuals may be the most effective strategy for self-preservation. Aggressive individuals can be emotionally draining and potentially dangerous, and if interactions consistently lead to emotional distress or conflict, it may be necessary to reevaluate the level of contact and establish stricter boundaries, including potentially cutting ties altogether if the situation warrants it.

Assertive communication and conflict resolution skills are essential for fostering productive interactions with aggressive personalities. Assertiveness training can help individuals express their needs, concerns, and boundaries confidently and effectively. Developing conflict resolution skills can enable individuals to navigate confrontations and disputes constructively and respectfully.

In conclusion, dealing with aggressive personalities requires a combination of awareness, assertiveness, and self-care. Recognizing different forms of aggression, such as verbal, physical, and passive-aggressive behavior, is essential for protecting one's well-being. Conflict resolution strategies, including active listening, empathy, and assertive communication, can help de-escalate confrontations and promote understanding. Setting and keeping boundaries is crucial for protecting one's autonomy and emotional health. Avoiding escalation and seeking support and self-care are vital for managing the stress and emotional toll of dealing with aggression. Ultimately, individuals must prioritize their well-being and protect themselves when faced with aggressive personalities.

The Know-It-All

Interacting with know-it-all individuals can be a challenging experience. These individuals often display an unwavering belief in their own knowledge and expertise, leading to frustration, conflict, and communication breakdowns with those around them. Know-it-alls tend to dominate conversations, dismiss alternative viewpoints, and resist input from others. In this section, we will explore the dynamics of dealing with know-it-alls, strategies for effective communication, and approaches for maintaining one's sanity and fostering constructive interactions.

One of the defining characteristics of know-it-all individuals is their constant need to assert their knowledge and expertise. They may interrupt conversations to offer unsolicited advice, correct others' statements, or monopolize discussions with their own opinions. Recognizing this behavior is the first step in dealing with know-it-alls. It is essential to maintain awareness of when a know-it-all dominates a conversation and be prepared for potential conflicts or disagreements.

Effective communication with know-it-alls requires a delicate balance of assertiveness and diplomacy. While confronting or challenging their assertions directly can be tempting, this approach often leads to resistance and defensiveness. Instead, individuals should aim to assert themselves calmly and respectfully, expressing their own opinions and expertise without dismissing the know-it-all's perspective entirely. Active listening and validation of the know-it-all's contributions, when appropriate, can help create a more receptive atmosphere for communication.

Recognizing the insecurity behind the know-it-all persona is essential for understanding their behavior. Know-it-alls often use their knowledge as a defense mechanism to mask feelings of inadequacy or insecurity. This recognition does not excuse their behavior but can help individuals approach interactions with empathy and patience. By addressing the underlying insecurity, it may be possible to foster more productive and collaborative conversations.

Setting boundaries is crucial when dealing with know-it-alls. Individuals should assert their right to express their own opinions and perspectives without fear of being dismissed or belittled. Establishing clear boundaries for communication, such as requesting equal airtime in conversations or asking the know-it-all to listen actively, can help create a more balanced and respectful interaction. Communicating boundaries assertively and consistently to ensure they are respected is important.

Choosing battles wisely is another strategy for managing interactions with know-it-alls. Not every instance of a know-it-all behavior requires a response or confrontation. Individuals should prioritize addressing know-it-all behavior when it hinders productive communication, disrupts relationships, or causes significant frustration. In less critical situations, letting minor instances of know-it- all behavior go without confrontation may be more effective.

Collaborative communication techniques can help bridge the gap in interactions with know-it-alls. These techniques emphasize active listening, empathy, and open-mindedness, fostering an environment where distinct perspectives are valued and respected. Encouraging the know-it-all to consider alternative viewpoints and engage in constructive dialogue can lead to more meaningful and productive interactions. Collaborative communication techniques can also help mitigate defensiveness and resistance on the part of the know-it-all.

Maintaining one's own self-esteem and self-worth is vital when dealing with know-it-alls. Their constant need to assert their knowledge can sometimes lead to feelings of inadequacy or self-doubt in others. Individuals should recognize that the know-it-all's behavior is a reflection of their own insecurities and not a valid judgment of others' worth or competence. Cultivating self-confidence and self-affirmation independently of the know-it-all's opinions is crucial for maintaining emotional well-being.

Sometimes, it may be necessary to limit contact with know-it-alls to protect one's sanity and well-being. Prolonged interactions with know-it-alls can be emotionally draining and frustrating. If conversations consistently lead to conflict or distress, individuals should consider whether the relationship or interaction is worth the toll it takes on their mental and emotional health. Limiting contact or setting boundaries around communication frequency may be necessary for self-preservation.

Support and self-care are vital when dealing with know-it-alls. Interacting with individuals who constantly assert their knowledge can be emotionally taxing. Seeking support from friends, family, or professionals can provide validation, guidance, and a sense of perspective. Engaging in self-care practices such as mindfulness, relaxation techniques, and therapy can help individuals manage the stress and emotional toll of dealing with know-it-alls.

Recognizing that changing a know-it-all's behavior is often challenging is essential. Know-it-alls may be unaware of how their behavior affects others or may be deeply ingrained in their need to assert their knowledge. Attempting to change their behavior may lead to resistance and defensiveness. Instead, individuals should focus on managing their own responses, fostering constructive communication, and setting boundaries to protect their well-being.

In conclusion, dealing with know-it-all individuals requires a combination of awareness, assertiveness, and self-care. Recognizing the characteristics of know-it-all behavior, such as constant assertion of knowledge and resistance to alternative viewpoints, is essential for effective communication. Collaborative communication techniques, setting boundaries, and choosing battles wisely can help mitigate conflicts and frustration in interactions with know-it-alls. It is important to maintain one's self-esteem independently of the know-it-all's opinions and consider limiting contact if interactions consistently lead to distress. Seeking support and practicing self-care are vital for managing the emotional toll of dealing with know-it-alls. Ultimately, individuals must prioritize their well-being and emotional health when faced with constant assertions of knowledge from others.

Complainer

Dealing with chronic complainers can be a challenging and draining experience. These individuals often have a penchant for focusing on the negative aspects of life, frequently venting their grievances and dissatisfaction with little regard for the impact on those around them. Complainers can create an atmosphere of negativity and frustration, which can lead to strained relationships and emotional exhaustion. In this section, we will explore the dynamics of dealing with chronic complainers, strategies for effective communication, and approaches for maintaining one's own well-being and fostering healthier interactions.

One of the defining characteristics of chronic complainers is their persistent and often excessive expression of dissatisfaction. They may frequently voice complaints about various aspects of their lives, ranging from work and relationships to personal challenges and inconveniences. Recognizing this behavior is the first step in dealing with complainers. It is essential to acknowledge when someone consistently dwells on negativity and to be prepared for potential conflicts or emotional exhaustion.

Effective communication with chronic complainers requires a delicate balance of empathy and assertiveness. While dismissing their grievances or offering solutions to their problems can be tempting, these approaches often lead to defensiveness and frustration. Instead, individuals should aim to listen actively and empathize with the complainer's feelings without necessarily agreeing with their perspective. Offering support and understanding can create a more conducive atmosphere for communication.

Understanding the underlying reasons behind chronic complaining is crucial for empathizing with complainers. Many chronic complainers use their complaints as a way to seek validation, attention, or empathy from others. Recognizing that their complaints may stem from unmet emotional needs can help individuals approach interactions with compassion and patience. By addressing the underlying emotional needs, it may be possible to foster more constructive and empathetic conversations.

Setting boundaries is essential when dealing with chronic complainers. Individuals should assert their right to maintain a positive and constructive environment and protect themselves from the constant influx of negativity. Establishing clear boundaries for communication, such as limiting the time spent discussing complaints or requesting a shift in conversation toward more positive topics, can help create a healthier and more balanced interaction. Consistently enforcing these boundaries is essential for maintaining one's own emotional well-being.

Choosing one's battles wisely is another strategy for managing interactions with chronic complainers. Not every complaint warrants a response or emotional investment. Individuals should prioritize addressing complaints that are genuinely important or directly impact their well-being. For less critical issues, letting minor complaints go without confrontation may be more effective, thereby conserving emotional energy and preventing unnecessary conflicts.

Fostering a solution-oriented mindset can help redirect chronic complainers toward more constructive conversations. While chronic complainers often focus on problems and grievances, encouraging them to consider possible solutions or strategies for improvement can be beneficial. Individuals can gently suggest alternative perspectives or inquire about potential actions that could alleviate their concerns. Shifting the conversation from dwelling on problems to exploring solutions can create a more positive and productive interaction.

Maintaining one's own emotional well-being is vital when dealing with chronic complainers. The constant exposure to negativity and complaints can take a toll on one's mental and emotional health. Individuals should prioritize self-care practices to manage the stress and emotional exhaustion that may result from these interactions. Engaging in activities that promote mindfulness, relaxation, and emotional resilience can help individuals maintain their well-being in the face of chronic complaining.

In some cases, it may be necessary to limit contact with chronic complainers to protect one's emotional health. Prolonged interactions with individuals who consistently focus on negativity can be emotionally draining and exhausting. Suppose conversations with chronic complainers consistently lead to frustration, stress, or emotional distress. In that case, individuals should consider whether the relationship or interaction is worth the toll it takes on their mental and emotional well-being. Limiting contact or setting boundaries around communication frequency may be necessary for self-preservation.

Support and self-care are vital when dealing with chronic complainers. Interacting with individuals who habitually express dissatisfaction can be emotionally taxing. Seeking support from friends, family, or professionals can provide validation, guidance, and a sense of perspective. Engaging in self-care practices such as mindfulness, relaxation techniques, and therapy can help individuals manage the stress and emotional toll of dealing with chronic complainers.

Recognizing that changing a chronic complainer's behavior is often challenging is essential. Chronic complainers may be unaware of how their behavior affects others or have ingrained habits of negativity. Attempting to change their behavior may lead to resistance and defensiveness. Instead, individuals should focus on managing their own responses, fostering empathetic communication, and setting boundaries to protect their well-being.

In conclusion, dealing with chronic complainers requires a combination of awareness, empathy, and self-care. Recognizing the characteristics of chronic complaining, such as persistent negativity and the expression of grievances, is essential for effective communication. Empathetic listening, validation, and support can create a more conducive atmosphere for interactions with chronic complainers. Setting and keeping boundaries is crucial for protecting one's emotional well-being and creating a healthier interaction. Choosing one's battles wisely, fostering a solution-oriented mindset, and keeping practices self-care are all strategies for managing the emotional toll of dealing with chronic complainers. Ultimately, individuals must prioritize their own emotional well-being and protect themselves when faced with chronic negativity from others.

CHAPTER X

Maintaining Long-Term Transformation

Relapse Prevention

Achieving long-term transformation in various aspects of life, whether it be overcoming addiction, adopting healthier habits, or managing a chronic condition, is a significant accomplishment. However, challenges and setbacks often mark the journey toward personal change. One of the most significant obstacles to long-term transformation is the risk of relapse—a return to old behaviors or patterns of thinking and acting that undermine progress. To maintain lasting transformation, individuals need to understand the nature of relapse, identify potential triggers, and implement effective relapse prevention strategies.

Relapse is a common occurrence on the path to long-term transformation. It occurs when individuals revert to their previous behaviors or habits, often undoing their progress. The nature of relapse can vary depending on the specific transformation goal. For instance, in addiction recovery, relapse involves a return to substance use after a period of abstinence. In weight management, relapse may involve regaining lost weight and reverting to unhealthy eating patterns. In mental health, relapse can manifest as a recurrence of symptoms or a decline in coping skills.

Preventing relapse requires an understanding of the factors that lead to it. Common triggers for relapse include stress, negative emotions, social pressure, exposure to environmental cues associated with the old behavior, and a lack of coping strategies. It's critical to understand that relapse is a typical aspect of the transformation process rather than an indication of failure. How individuals respond to relapse determines their ultimate success in maintaining long-term change.

Relapse prevention strategies are created to help individuals recognize and manage triggers, develop coping skills, and maintain their commitment to long-term transformation. These strategies can be adapted to various transformation goals but share common principles that apply across the board.

One fundamental aspect of relapse prevention is building self-awareness. People must be aware of their triggers and the warning indicators that point to a possible relapse. This necessitates open self-evaluation and a readiness to face unsettling feelings and ideas. Self-awareness helps individuals anticipate and prepare for potential challenges.

Another critical component of relapse prevention is the development of coping strategies. Identifying healthier ways to deal with stress, negative emotions, and external pressures is essential. Coping strategies can include mindfulness techniques, problem-solving skills, seeking social support, participating in physical activity, or pursuing creative outlets. These strategies provide alternative ways to respond to triggers and reduce the likelihood of relapse.

Social support plays a vital role in relapse prevention. A network of friends, family, or support groups can offer motivation, responsibility, and a feeling of community. Talking to people who are traveling a similar path about your experiences and difficulties can be very beneficial. Support systems help individuals stay motivated and provide a safety net when facing relapse.

Incorporating relapse prevention strategies into daily routines is essential. Consistency and commitment are key factors in maintaining long-term transformation. Individuals should develop a relapse prevention plan that outlines their triggers, coping strategies, and support systems. This plan serves as a guide to navigating challenging situations and serves as a reminder of their commitment to change.

Furthermore, practicing self-compassion is essential in relapse prevention. Acknowledging that setbacks are a natural part of the transformation process and that everyone makes mistakes is crucial. Self-criticism and guilt can hinder progress, while self-compassion fosters resilience and a positive mindset. Individuals must treat themselves with the same kindness and understanding they would provide to a friend facing a similar challenge. Maintaining motivation and a sense of purpose is also integral to relapse prevention. Setting clear, realistic goals and regularly reviewing progress can help individuals stay focused and motivated. Celebrating achievements, no matter how small, strengthens the sense of accomplishment and reinforces the commitment to long-term transformation.

It's important to note that relapse prevention is an ongoing process. It doesn't end when an individual achieves their initial transformation goals. Rather, it becomes a lifelong commitment to maintaining the positive changes made. As individuals progress in their journey, they may need to adapt their relapse prevention strategies to address new challenges and circumstances.

In addiction recovery, for example, individuals often learn to identify and manage high-risk situations that could lead to relapse. This may involve avoiding certain people, places, or triggers associated with substance use. In weight management, individuals may continuously monitor their eating habits and physical activity to prevent gradual weight regain. To maintain their mental health, people can engage in self-care practices and schedule frequent check-ins with mental health specialists.

The role of professional guidance in relapse prevention should not be underestimated. Mental health counselors, addiction specialists, nutritionists, and other experts can provide valuable support and guidance tailored to an individual's specific needs. They can help individuals develop personalized relapse prevention plans and offer strategies for addressing unique challenges.

In conclusion, relapse prevention is a crucial element of maintaining long-term transformation. While relapse is a common part of the transformation process, it doesn't signify failure. Rather, it provides an opportunity for individuals to learn and strengthen their commitment to change. Understanding the factors that contribute to relapse, building self-awareness, developing coping strategies, seeking social support, and practicing self-compassion are all essential elements of successful relapse prevention. It's important to recognize that relapse prevention is a lifelong commitment to maintaining positive changes and adapting strategies to evolving circumstances. Individuals can achieve and sustain long-term transformation in their lives with dedication and the right support.

Building Support Networks

Achieving long-term transformation in any aspect of life, whether it involves overcoming addiction, adopting healthier habits, managing a chronic condition, or pursuing personal growth, often relies heavily on the support of others. Building and maintaining a strong support network is essential for individuals seeking to sustain positive changes over the long term. These networks provide encouragement, accountability, and resources to help individuals navigate the difficulties and setbacks that inevitably arise on the path to transformation.

Support networks come in various forms, including friends, family, support groups, mentors, therapists, and communities. They serve as a crucial source of emotional support, guidance, and motivation. The significance of these networks cannot be overstated, as they play a central role in fostering resilience and sustaining progress.

One primary function of a support network is to provide emotional support. Transformation journeys often involve moments of self-doubt, frustration, and discouragement. During these times, the presence of supportive individuals who offer empathy, validation, and understanding can make a world of difference. Sharing one's struggles and triumphs with a trusted support network allows individuals to process their emotions and gain perspective on their journey.

Accountability is another critical aspect of a support network. Having individuals who hold us accountable for our actions and commitments can be a powerful motivator for maintaining long-term change. Accountability partners or mentors can help individuals stay on track by tracking progress, setting goals, and providing gentle reminders when necessary. The knowledge that someone is watching and rooting for our success can serve as a potent incentive to stay dedicated to transformation goals.

Practical assistance and resources from a support network can also be invaluable. Whether it involves providing transportation, childcare, access to information, or financial support, the tangible assistance from others can remove barriers and facilitate the pursuit of transformation goals. Support networks can help individuals access the tools and resources they need to succeed.

Support networks often provide a sense of belonging and connectedness. Engaging with others who share the same experiences and goals can reduce feelings of isolation and create a sense of community. This sense of belonging can be particularly meaningful for individuals facing challenges related to addiction recovery, chronic illness, or mental health, where stigma and misunderstanding may contribute to feelings of isolation.

Effective communication is a cornerstone of building and maintaining support networks. Individuals should actively reach out to friends, family, or communities that align with their transformation goals. Expressing their needs, goals, and challenges is essential for enlisting support and collaboration. It's important to foster open and honest communication within the support network, ensuring that everyone involved is on the same page and understands their role.

Boundaries within support networks are equally crucial. While a support network should be a source of encouragement and assistance, individuals must also establish clear boundaries to protect their well-being. This may involve setting limits on the type or amount of support they are willing to accept or specifying their expectations regarding privacy and confidentiality. Healthy boundaries ensure that support networks remain constructive and respectful.

Diversity within a support network can enhance its effectiveness. Seeking support from a variety of sources, such as friends, family, professionals, and support groups, can provide a well-rounded and comprehensive network. Different individuals or groups may offer unique perspectives, resources, and forms of support that cater to various aspects of an individual's transformation journey.

Support networks should be flexible and adaptive to evolving needs. As individuals progress on their transformation journey, their support needs may change. It's essential to assess and adjust the composition and structure of the support network as circumstances change. For example, someone in addiction recovery may initially benefit from a support group but later find that individual therapy better meets their needs.

The reciprocity of support networks is a fundamental aspect of their sustainability. Individuals should recognize that support networks involve a give-and-take dynamic, not one-sided relationships. Just as individuals receive support, they should also be willing to offer support to others when the opportunity arises. This reciprocity strengthens the bonds within the network and fosters a sense of collective empowerment.

Support networks should be nurtured and maintained regularly. Building a support network is not a one-time effort but an ongoing process. Individuals should invest time and effort into nurturing their relationships, staying connected, and expressing gratitude for the support they receive. Regular check-ins and updates help keep the network engaged and informed about one's progress.

Cultivating resilience within a support network is essential for facing challenges and setbacks. Transformation journeys are rarely linear, and setbacks are a natural part of the process. A resilient support network can provide the encouragement and guidance needed to bounce back from setbacks, learn from experiences, and continue the journey toward long-term transformation.

In conclusion, building and keeping a strong support network is essential for maintaining long-term transformation. These networks provide emotional support, accountability, practical assistance, a sense of belonging, and resources that empower individuals to navigate the difficulties and setbacks that arise on their journey. Effective communication, boundaries, and reciprocity are critical components of a successful support network. By actively cultivating and nurturing these networks, individuals can enhance their resilience, sustain their progress, and achieve lasting transformation in their lives.

Personal Growth

Long-term transformation is a journey that extends far beyond the initial stages of change. Whether it involves breaking free from addiction, improving one's mental health, adopting healthier habits, or achieving personal and professional goals, maintaining lasting transformation requires continuous personal growth and development. This section will explore the integral role of personal growth in sustaining long-term transformation, the mindset and practices that support it, and the benefits it brings to individuals on their transformative journeys.

At its core, personal growth involves a commitment to self-improvement and self-awareness. It is the process of expanding one's knowledge, skills, and perspective, often driven by a desire for positive change and self-realization. In the context of long-term transformation, personal growth acts as the foundation upon which individuals build and maintain their newfound behaviors, habits, and outlook on life.

A growth mindset, as coined by psychologist Carol Dweck, is a fundamental element of personal growth. It entails believing that dedication and hard work can develop abilities and intelligence. Individuals having a growth mindset tend to embrace challenges, persevere through setbacks, and view failures as opportunities for learning and improvement. This mindset is particularly valuable when facing the inevitable challenges and setbacks encountered on the path to long-term transformation.

Self-awareness is another critical component of personal growth. It involves deeply understanding one's thoughts, feelings, behaviors, and motivations. Self-aware individuals can determine their strengths and weaknesses, recognize their triggers, and pinpoint areas in which they need to grow. This self-knowledge is essential for making informed choices and taking intentional actions that align with long-term transformation goals.

Continuous learning and skill development are central to personal growth. Individuals seeking long-term transformation must be open to acquiring new knowledge and skills that support their goals. This may involve formal education, self-directed learning, seeking mentorship, or exploring new experiences. Learning expands one's capabilities and enhances adaptability and resilience in the face of change.

Goal setting and goal-oriented behaviors are pivotal in personal growth and long-term transformation. Setting clear and an achievable goals provides a sense of direction and purpose. These goals act as milestones along the transformation journey, helping individuals measure their progress and stay motivated. Regularly reviewing and adjusting goals ensures that individuals remain aligned with their evolving aspirations.

Resilience is a quality closely linked to personal growth. It is the ability to bounce back from adversity and adapt positively to change. Resilient individuals view challenges as possibilites for growth and maintain a sense of hope and optimism. Building resilience involves developing effective coping strategies, cultivating a strong support network, and nurturing emotional well-being. Self-

discipline is a key trait that supports personal growth and long-term transformation. It involves the ability to exert self-control, stay focused on goals, and resist immediate gratification for the sake of long-term benefits.

Self-discipline helps individuals maintain consistent behaviors and make choices that align with their transformation objectives. Developing self-discipline often requires practice, commitment, and managing distractions and temptations.

Embracing change is a crucial aspect of personal growth. Transformation itself is a process of change, and individuals must be willing to adapt to new circumstances and experiences. This may entail letting go of old beliefs or habits, accepting uncertainty, and embracing opportunities for personal development. A willingness to change is often a prerequisite for achieving and sustaining long-term transformation.

Acceptance and self-compassion are integral to personal growth. Transformation journeys are rarely without setbacks or moments of self-doubt. During these times, individuals must practice self-compassion by treating themselves with kindness and an understanding rather than harsh self-criticism. Accepting that relapses or temporary setbacks are part of the process allows individuals to learn from their experiences and continue their journey with renewed determination.

The process of personal growth is ongoing and iterative. It involves self-reflection, learning, and self-improvement throughout one's life. Individuals should prioritize self-growth as a lifelong endeavor rather than a one-time achievement. Embracing the idea that personal growth is a continuous process reinforces the commitment to long-term transformation and the development of resilience in the face of adversity.

The benefits of personal growth in maintaining long-term transformation are numerous. First and foremost, personal growth enhances an individual's ability to adapt and navigate change effectively. This adaptability is essential when facing unexpected challenges or triggers that may threaten the sustainability of transformation efforts.

Furthermore, personal growth fosters a sense of empowerment and self-efficacy. As individuals acquire new skills, knowledge, and coping strategies, they gain confidence in managing their lives and overcoming obstacles. This increased self-efficacy fuels motivation and determination to maintain long-term transformation. Personal growth also deepens self-awareness and emotional intelligence. Individuals who engage in self-reflection and personal development become more attuned to their emotions, needs, and motivations. This heightened self-awareness allows for better decision-making, increased empathy, and improved interpersonal relationships.

Additionally, personal growth enhances problem-solving and critical thinking abilities. Individuals aiming to expand their knowledge and skills become better equipped to analyze complex situations, make informed decisions, and overcome obstacles. This capacity for effective problem-solving is invaluable when facing the challenges of long-term transformation.

Lastly, personal growth contributes to a sense of purpose and fulfillment. As individuals continuously work toward self-improvement and align their actions with their values and aspirations, they often experience a more profound sense of meaning in their lives. This feeling of direction can serve as a strong incentive to sustain long-term change.

In conclusion, personal growth is an integral and ongoing component of maintaining long-term transformation. It involves developing a growth mindset, fostering self-awareness, continuous learning and skill development, goal setting, resilience, self-discipline, and a willingness to embrace change. Personal growth empowers individuals to adapt, navigate challenges, and develop the resilience necessary for sustaining transformation efforts. The benefits of personal growth extend to enhanced adaptability, self-efficacy, self-awareness, problem- solving abilities, and a profound sense of purpose and fulfillment. Individuals can achieve and maintain long- lasting positive change in their lives by prioritizing personal growth as an essential aspect of their transformation journey.

CONCLUSION

In "Beyond Conflict: Transforming Relationships with Difficult Individuals," we embarked on a journey of self-discovery and interpersonal growth. This book has illuminated the path to understanding, empathy, and transformation in the face of challenging relationships. As we conclude our exploration, reflecting on the key takeaways and the overarching message of this transformative journey is essential.

Throughout the pages of this book, we delved into the intricate landscape of difficult individuals, recognizing that behind their challenging behaviors lie complex stories, unmet needs, and personal struggles. We learned that understanding these individuals, acknowledging their humanity, and recognizing common traits and triggers can pave the way for more compassionate interactions.

Moreover, we explored the profound impact of conflict on individuals, on their emotional and mental health, and also on their physical well-being. Recognizing the far-reaching consequences of unresolved conflict, we embraced the importance of empathy, effective communication, and conflict resolution techniques as tools for fostering healthier relationships.

In the pursuit of personal growth and transformation, we examined strategies for self-reflection, emotional intelligence, and active listening. We discovered that the power of empathy and nonviolent communication transcends conflicts, bridging the divide between difficult individuals and ourselves. Furthermore, we harnessed the potential of self-reflection and boundary-setting to protect our well-being while maintaining a compassionate mindset.

The case studies provided in this book offered real-world examples of individuals who navigated the challenging waters of difficult relationships, showcasing the transformative potential of understanding, empathy, and effective communication. These stories of healing and reconciliation demonstrated that positive change and growth are possible even in the most challenging circumstances.

As we conclude our journey, it is essential to acknowledge that transformation is an ongoing process. The insights and strategies shared in "Beyond Conflict" serve as valuable tools in the toolkit of personal growth and relationship transformation. They remind us that change is possible and a continuous and evolving endeavor.
In our pursuit of healthier relationships and personal growth, we must remember that while we cannot control the actions or behaviors of others, we have agency over our own responses and choices. Through self-awareness, empathy, and a commitment to ongoing personal growth, we can navigate the complex terrain of difficult relationships with grace and resilience.

Ultimately, "Beyond Conflict: Transforming Relationships with Difficult Individuals" invites us to transcend the limitations of conflict and strife, embracing the transformative power of understanding, empathy, and effective communication. It reminds us that, in the face of adversity, we cannot only change ourselves but also inspire change in others, creating a ripple effect of compassion and healing that extends far beyond our immediate relationships. As we carry the lessons of this book forward, may we continue to journey beyond conflict and towards a world of deeper connection, understanding, and transformation.

Thank you for buying and reading/ listening to our book. If you found this book useful/ helpful please take a few minutes and leave a review on the platform where you purchased our book. Your feedback matters greatly to us.